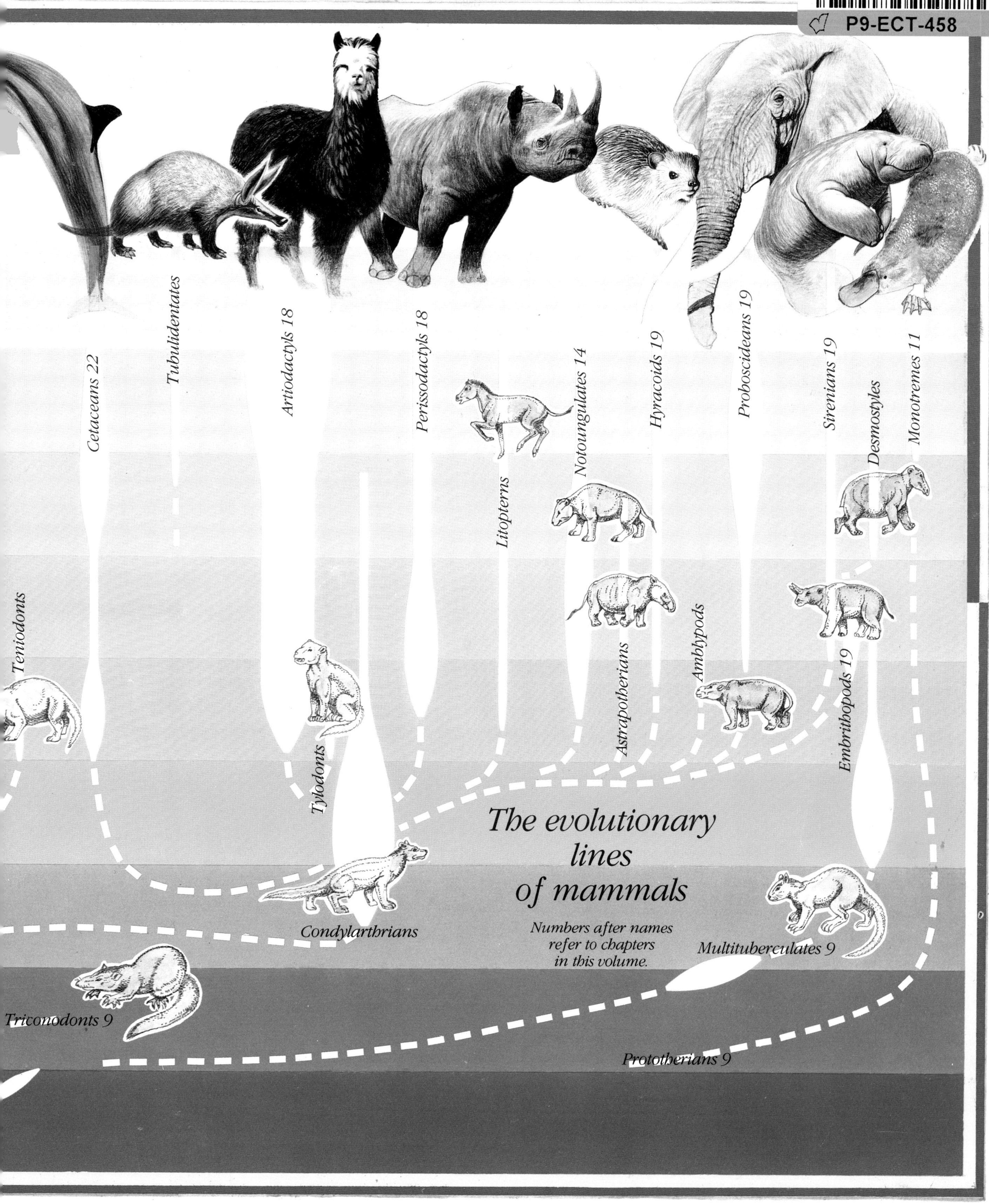

The evolutionary lines of mammals

Numbers after names refer to chapters in this volume.

Cetaceans 22

Tubulidentates

Artiodactyls 18

Perissodactyls 18

Litopterns

Notoungulates 14

Hyracoids 19

Proboscideans 19

Sirenians 19

Desmostyles

Monotremes 11

Teniodonts

Tylodonts

Astrapotherians

Amblypods

Embrithopods 19

Condylarthrians

Multituberculates 9

Triconodonts 9

Prototherians 9

THE HISTORY OF LIFE ON EARTH

MAMMALS

© 1987 English-language edition by Facts On File, Inc.
460 Park Avenue South, New York, NY 10016

© 1987 Editoriale Jaca Book SpA, Milano

editorial coordination

CATERINA LONGANESI

CONTENTS

1. The Origin of Mammals
2. General Features: Homeothermy and Body Hair
3. Sense Organs and Respiration
4. Sense of Smell, Color, Camouflage
5. Embryo and Suckling
6. Intelligence, Learning, Living in Groups
7. Feeding
8. Movement
9. The Evolutionary Branches of Mammals
10. The Unsettled History of Mammals
11. Monotremes
12. American Marsupials
13. Australian Marsupials
14. The Great Extinct Placental Mammals
15. Insectivores, Edentates and Pholidota
16. Chiropters
17. Rodents and Lagomorphs
18. Perissodactyls and Artiodactyls
19. Proboscideans, Hyracoids, Sirenians
20. Fissiped Carnivores
21. Pinniped Carnivores
22. Cetaceans
23. The Primates Appear
24. The Prosimians
25. Platyrrhine Monkeys
26. Catarrhine Monkeys
27. The Road to Man
28. Homo
29. Modern Man

Library of Congress Cataloging-in-Publication Data

Minelli, G.
   Mammals.

   (History of life on earth)
   Translation of: I mammiferi.
   Summary: Discusses evolution of vertebrates
on earth from earliest life forms.
      1. Mammals—Evolution—Juvenile literature.
2. Mammals, Fossil—Juvenile literature. [1. Mammals—
Evolution. 2. Evolution] I. Title. II. Series.
QL708.5.M5613   596'.038   87-15612
ISBN 0-8160-1560-0

color separation by
Carlo Scotti, Milano
photosetting by
Elle Due, Milano
printed and bound in Italy by
Tipolitografia G. Canale & C. Spa, Torino

MAMMALS

Giuseppe Minelli

Professor of Comparative Anatomy
University of Bologna, Italy

illustrated by
Remo Berselli and Marzio Tamer

the "History of Life on Earth" series
is conceived, designed and produced by
Jaca Book

Facts On File Publications
New York, New York ● Oxford, England

1. THE ORIGIN OF MAMMALS

The class to which we belong began its development and expansion about 65 million years ago, after the disappearance of the dinosaurs. With the earth cleared of the large and small reptiles that had dominated it for almost the whole of the Mesozoic Era, the extremely rapid evolution of the mammals began. But the origins of the class lay much further back in time.

PRECURSORS OF THE MAMMALS

The subject has been dealt with in greater detail in the *Reptiles* volume in this series. In Chapters 13 and 14 the therapsids, also known as "mammal-like reptiles," were examined. In the Permian-Triassic Periods the therapsids held sway over the whole of the earth, which consisted at that time of a single supercontinent. They made up 80% of living reptiles and included herbivorous forms as large as an ox and carnivorous forms no bigger than a large wolf. Their rule came to an end with the arrival of a new group of reptiles, the thecodont archosaurs, which installed themselves in the same ecological niche. The new thecodont archosaurs also gave rise to the dinosaurs, highly specialized reptiles that, among other things, were the first animals to adopt the erect posture with a bipedal gait, considerably increasing the speed at which they could run.

THE THERIODONT THERAPSIDS

Not all the therapsid reptiles became extinct on the appearance of the thecodonts; some forms, perhaps less specialized, survived and gave rise to mammals.

When reconstructing the history of vertebrates it is often difficult to find intermediate forms between one class and another. Thus we saw, for instance, an abrupt leap between the form of a crossopterygian fish and that of an amphibian, or between an ostracoderm and a placoderm, in the transition from the reptile to the

mammal; conversely, there is an abundance of intermediary forms, to the point where there is still doubt today over whether many species were actually reptiles or should have been classed as mammals. One suborder of therapsids in particular, the theriodonts, had a marked tendency to acquire new mammal-like features. Two evolutionary lines of these theriodonts, the ictidosaurians and tritylodons, accumulated such a large quantity of mammalian features that it becomes arbitrary to go on calling them reptiles. In fact they had a skeletal structure similar to that of mammals; they were able to regulate their body temperature and may even have been covered with fur to reduce heat loss; they were able to chew, something that no other reptile can do; they had a good sense of smell and often forward-facing wide eyes. It is natural to ask at this point why some mammalian features appeared in these reptiles, and in these alone. There are several possible answers: for some researchers the appearance of the new features was the expression of genetic information already present in the therapsids that was in the end only able to emerge in the theriodonts. For others, the answer is more commonplace: the presence and the overwhelming power of the dinosaurs not only led to massive slaughter among the therapsids but also drove a number of them to take refuge in the only environment still available: the nocturnal habitat.

ADAPTATION TO THE DARK

The first animals about whose mammalian nature there is no doubt, whose appearance dates back to the Jurassic Period, are all adapted to live in a poorly lit or dark environment. The adaptation to nocturnal life has left its mark on the entire class even though, with the disappearance of the dinosaurs, the rapid expansion of the mammals led them to reconquer the diurnal habitat.

The earliest mammals date back to about 200 million years ago. Small in size and similar in appearance to rats, they lived alongside the powerful dinosaurs for a long time; pushed into the background, they occupied the same habitat at night. They were timid little creatures that roamed the undergrowth in search of insects. What we see is a reconstruction since the only fossil remains of early mammals are a few teeth and incomplete skulls.

Today — Snakes, Lizards, Monitors, Geckos, Iguanas, etc.

1.8 Recent Era

Tertiary Era

65

Cretaceous

136

Jurassic — OPHIDIANS AND SAURIANS

195

Triassic — DINOSAURS AND PTEROSAURS

225

Permian

280

Carboniferous

345 million years ago

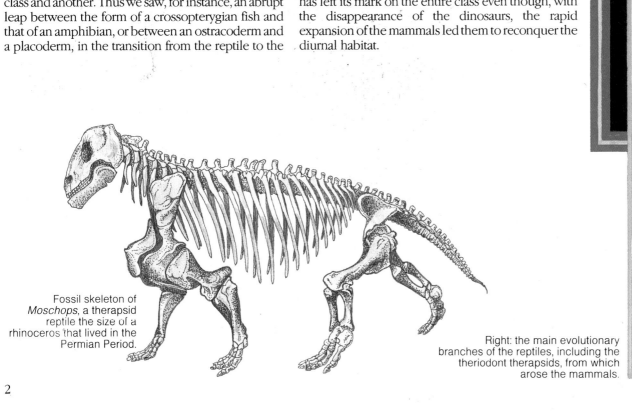

Fossil skeleton of *Moschops*, a therapsid reptile the size of a rhinoceros that lived in the Permian Period.

Right: the main evolutionary branches of the reptiles, including the theriodont therapsids, from which arose the mammals.

2

Tortoises and turtles

Crocodiles

toward the MAMMALS

LORICATES

CHELONIANS

THECODONT ARCHOSAURS

THERIODONT THERAPSIDS

COTYLOSAURS

PELICOSAURS

large and forward-facing eye

hard palate

broad nostrils

Fossil skull of *Tritilodon*, a theriodont therapsid from the end of the Triassic Period. The numerous mammalian features of this reptile are indicated.

lower jaw made out of a single bone

teeth differentiated for tearing and grinding

3

Mammals have bodies covered with fur. Some domestic species have a long and thick woolen coat used by man to make warm clothing.

Angora goat

Perhaps hair evolved from the scales of reptiles. Even today the armadillo is covered with horny scales during the first few weeks of life, beneath which grow tactile bristles. Left: an adult armadillo. Below: a detail of the skin of a newborn animal.

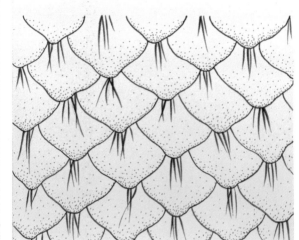

Nine-banded armadillo

2. GENERAL FEATURES: HOMEOTHERMY AND BODY HAIR

The major differences in structure and organization between a reptile and a mammal are partly the result of the latter's adaptation to poor light or darkness. From the appearance of the first mammals in the Jurassic Period until the extinction of the dinosaurs, over a period of 110-120 million years, our class acquired and perfected many modes of adaptation in order to survive in a difficult environment and one that was usually ignored by reptiles and birds: the night.

HOMEOTHERMY

In the first place, in darkness it was no longer possible to count on the benefits and warmth of the sun's rays. Hence it was extremely useful, almost indispensable, for the organism to be able to produce and conserve heat.

Of all living beings today, only birds and mammals are homeotherms, or warm-blooded animals, that is, they regulate their body temperatures to setpoints of 106° F (41° C) and 98.6° F (37° C) respectively. In previous volumes the hypothesis has been put forward that this capacity was also to be found among reptiles, both in the therapsids, from which the mammals arose, and in the dinosaurs, from which the birds evolved. To put into practice this function, which makes it possible to live, feed and reproduce fairly independently of the outside temperature, the animal requires a heating plant to produce heat and systems to regulate this production, by warming up or cooling down, as well, of course, as a system of overall control.

Heat is produced by the metabolism of every cell; in a mammal, roughly 40% of the heat is derived from the muscles, another 35% from the liver and the remaining 25% from the other parts of the body. The thyroid hormone is responsible for increasing or decreasing this production according to the requirements of the body.

PROTECTION FROM THE COLD

As the environment cools, at night for instance, the mammal has to prevent the loss of heat from its own body. This becomes more urgent as the external temperature drops and when the body size of the animal is small. It has already been shown, in the *Dinosaurs and Birds* volume in this series, how birds developed feathers to insulate the body from heat loss. In mammals, body hair is derived from the layers of the skin; not exclusive to mammals, body hair can

4

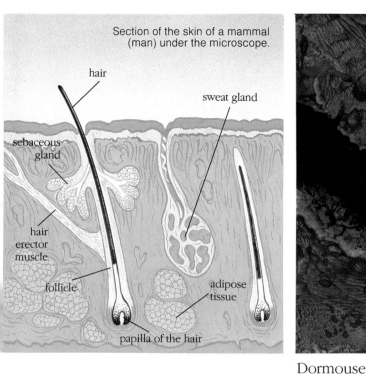

Section of the skin of a mammal (man) under the microscope.

hair

sweat gland

sebaceous gland

hair erector muscle

follicle

adipose tissue

papilla of the hair

Dormouse

At the beginning of the cold season the dormouse, a rodent that lives in Europe, digs itself an underground lair, lines it with grass and the remains of its last meal, curls up into a ball and falls into a state of profound torpor, from which it will awake in spring.

be found also in extinct thermoregulated reptiles, such as pterosaurs. It may have originated as a sense organ, as we shall see in the next Chapter, and may have been present along with scales. With the loss of the latter, body hair, growing longer and becoming an outer covering, or fur, provided good protection against the cold with the layer of air trapped within it.

PROTECTION FROM THE HEAT

An environment warmer than the body or intense physical effort (running or fighting) may lead to an excessive production of heat by an animal's muscles. A cooling system has to come into play in both cases. In the majority of mammals, this consists of sweat glands distributed in the skin. These supply a watery solution—sweat—whose evaporation cools down the whole body. However, not all mammals have sweat glands. For instance, many carnivores, such as dogs and cats, lose heat by panting: breathing becomes faster and the moisture which dampens the inner walls of the mouth evaporates, thus reducing the body heat.

HIBERNATION

In some species of mammals, the problem of survival under highly unfavorable climatic conditions is solved by hibernation. During such periods, the animal reduces its metabolic rate, allowing its body temperature to fall to a minimum and slowing down its heartbeat and its respiration. Under these conditions the animal lives on its body-fat reserves until food becomes available when the weather improves.

Red fox

Mammals are warm-blooded animals; that is, they maintain a constant body temperature independently of the climate of the environment in which they live. In this way many species are able to remain active in winter as well as summer.

5

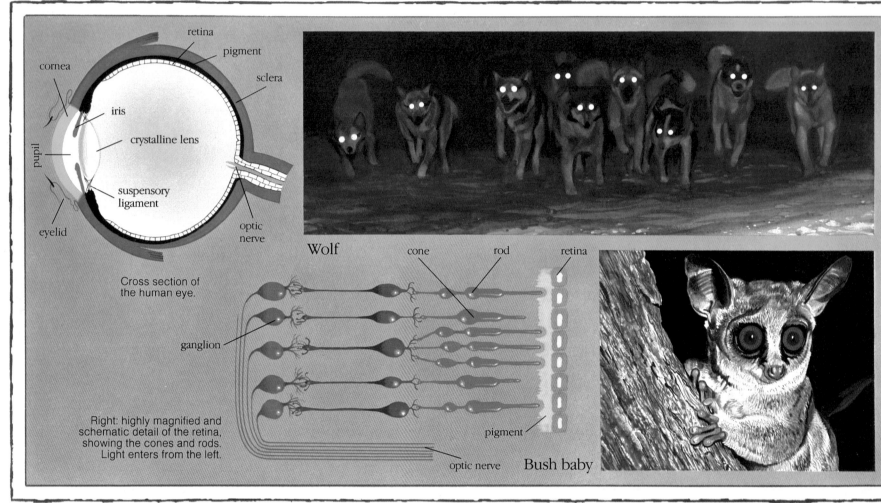

cornea
retina
pigment
sclera
iris
crystalline lens
pupil
suspensory ligament
eyelid
optic nerve

Cross section of the human eye.

Wolf

cone
rod
retina

ganglion

Right: highly magnified and schematic detail of the retina, showing the cones and rods. Light enters from the left.

pigment

optic nerve

Bush baby

The eye of the mammal provides evidence of its origin as a nocturnal animal. Some species, such as the wolf, have crystals behind the retina that reflect even the weakest light signals and project them out of the eye again: this creates the impression that their eyes glow in the dark. The bush baby, a nocturnal insect hunter and African member of the lemur family, has very large eyes.

3. SENSE ORGANS AND RESPIRATION

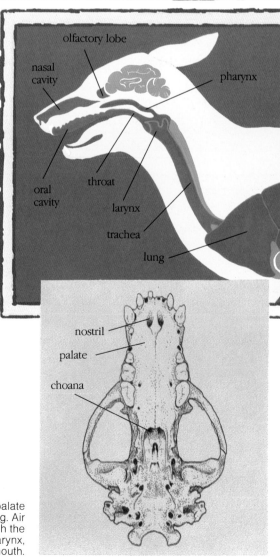

olfactory lobe
nasal cavity
pharynx
oral cavity
throat
larynx
trachea
lung

nostril
palate
choana

Without a doubt, the structures which, in the passage from reptiles to mammals, have undergone the most profound and surprising modifications in the process of adaptation to the nocturnal habitat are the sense organs.

THE EYE

This sense organ, which plays a fundamental role in the behavior of most reptiles and birds, loses importance in mammals. Its size, compared with the whole of the body, is generally modest, except for some arboreal prosimians, like bush babies. As their ancestors lived in dark surroundings, mammals have eyes which focus in front—like owls, also nocturnal animals; this permits a binocular vision and the ability to recognize patterns and shapes even in the faintest light. The light-sensitive part of the eye's retina is made up of two types of cells: the cones, squat in shape, can detect very intense colored light, while the more slender rods respond only to dull light and are responsible for perceiving black and white images. In most mammals, even in diurnal ones, the rods predominate, bearing witness to the long evolution in

the dark of this class. The readaptation to the bright light of the day may be too recent to have allowed the cones to return in force. In many nocturnal species, such as wolves, at the back of the retina there are crystals that reflect light and send it back to cones and rods, thus improving the efficiency of sight. This peculiarity gives a sinister glow to the animal's eyes in the dark, since the light that enters is concentrated and reflected out again.

THE EAR

Compared with the reptile's ear, this sense organ has deeply changed and improved in mammals, acquiring greater sensitivity to a broader spectrum of perceptible sound waves.

The ear of amphibians (see the corresponding volume in this series, Chapter 9), reptiles, or birds has a small bone (stapes) that transmits sound waves to

Skull of a bear seen from below. The bony palate permits simultaneous chewing and breathing. Air enters from the nostrils and passes through the choanas directly into the pharynx, bypassing the mouth.

6

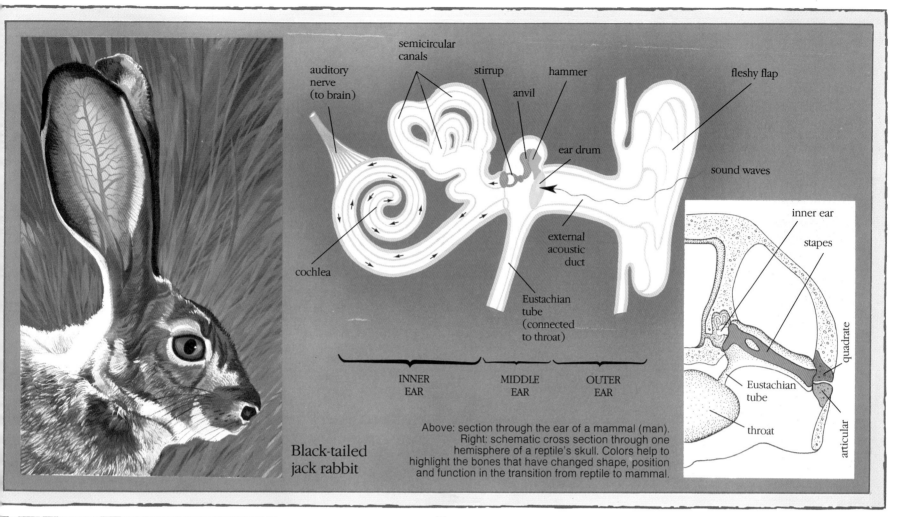

Black-tailed jack rabbit

Above: section through the ear of a mammal (man). Right: schematic cross section through one hemisphere of a reptile's skull. Colors help to highlight the bones that have changed shape, position and function in the transition from reptile to mammal.

The mammalian ear is characterized not only by its ossicles and long cochlea, but also by its external fleshy flap which in some animals lacking offensive weapons, such as the hare, is extremely large and can be moved so as to convey sound waves more efficiently toward the ear drum.

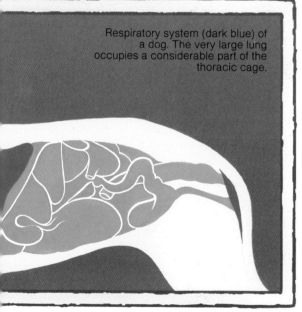

Respiratory system (dark blue) of a dog. The very large lung occupies a considerable part of the thoracic cage.

Tabby cat

The nose and eyes of the cat are surrounded by long tactile hairs known as vibrissae, which function as sense organs.

the inner ear. Mammals, on the other hand, have a middle ear with three small bones (stirrup, anvil, hammer), which amplify the sound waves. These three bones have different origins: the stirrup derives from the stapes; the anvil derives from the quadrate, a bone which links the lower jaw with the skull, and the hammer originates from the articular bone of the lower jaw. Hence the three new bones of mammals' ears are adaptations of bones that already existed in reptiles, but which had other functions. This modification is one of the most extraordinary examples of the great malleability of living organisms and of the enormous possibilities for adaptation offered by evolution. The part where the actual perception of sound occurs is the cochlea, in the inner ear, a spiral structure abounding in nerve cells. The length of the cochlea varies in different species of mammals: the longer it is, the broader the spectrum of wavelengths that are perceptible. Human beings, for example, are unable to hear the very high frequency sound waves that can be detected by the long cochlea of the dog or mouse. Another characteristic of mammals is the outer ear, varying in size and capable of movement, allowing it to be oriented towards the sound source so as to pick up the faintest of signals. The ear, rather than the eye, is a highly important sense organ for a mammal; its evolution and

specialization is a consequence of the long period of development undergone by our class in an environment where only sound could serve as a reliable signal for predator and prey alike.

HAIR AS A SENSE ORGAN

Besides insulating the body from heat loss, the hair acts as a sense organ as well. Long and rigid hairs are to be found on the heads of many mammals that lead a nocturnal existence or live in poorly lit burrows. The roots of these hairs are provided with an abundance of nerves, allowing them to function as sense organs, warning of the presence of obstacles. All hairs have this sensitivity, but it is intensified in these animals by exceptional length and rigidity.

RESPIRATION

The high rate of metabolism that results in a greater production of heat as well as an increased sensitivity in the animal requires a considerable consumption of oxygen and continual ventilation of the lungs. Compared with those of other classes, mammals' lungs are very voluminous and lie in cavities in the chest. Since it is impossible to chew and breathe at the same time with the typically reptilian mouth, through which both the respiratory and the alimentary tract pass, a continuous bony septum, the palate, separates the two tracts in mammals. In this way the two indispensable functions can be carried on simultaneously.

Left: olfactory membrane under the microscope.

Striped skunk

Axis deer

Pheasant

Labrador retriever

Grizzly bear

Diagram of the route followed by a Labrador retriever on the scent trail of a pheasant.

Pheasant

Labrador retriever

Many mammals have a highly developed sense of smell. Some species use it to track their prey on land, such as the hunting dog, or in water, such as the bear which also feeds on fish. Other animals, such as deer, leave odorous signals for their enemies or friends, marking their territory with the secretion from a gland located beneath their eye. Yet others, like the skunk, defend themselves from aggressors by spraying them with an evil-smelling and irritating liquid.

4. SENSE OF SMELL, COLOR, CAMOUFLAGE

OLFACTORY SIGNALS

Since visual signals are ineffective in the dark or in a dimly lit environment, the sense of smell has undergone exceptional development in mammals. In the skin of most mammals there is a wide range of scent glands situated in different parts of the body (either on the head, or in proximity to the genitals, or on the feet), whose secretions send precise messages to individuals of the same species. In general, the odor messages emitted by these glands serve two functions: either the marking of a territory for hunting or grazing, or as a signal of sexual maturity.

Both signals are very important to the survival of the species: the marking of territory, carried out in very

different ways (for example by placing on vegetation a tarry substance from a gland beneath the eye as deer and gazelles do, or urinating here and there as many carnivores do), helps to identify and reassure those who belong to the same species, and to warn strangers to stay out. The signals of sexual lure are very important as they improve the chances of mating between males and females, especially if they lead a solitary life. Sexual signals are released only when the gametes (and the eggs in particular) are mature, during a short period of the year, the one most suitable for reproduction; at other times the absence of olfactory signals annuls all sexual stimulation.

Odor can also be used as a defensive weapon. A good example is the skunk, well known for its foetid

secretion, ejected forcibly from the anal glands, which has irritant properties and is an effective deterrent to would-be predators.

THE SENSE OF SMELL

In step with the evolution of scent glands, the system of perception of odors is particularly efficient in mammals. Most mammals' behavior is guided by the sense of smell that can condition the whole of their activity. The nostrils of mammals are often large and open onto nasal cavities filled with olfactory membrane. However along with these sensitive noses (macrosmatics) there are some mammals with a poor

8

Chapman's zebra

Short-tailed weasel

engal tiger

The tiger and the zebra, a carnivore and an African herbivore, have in common a coat with light and dark stripes, which provides them with effective camouflage in vegetation or in the twilight.

Seven-colored tanager

Siamese fighting fish

Some mammals that live in regions covered with snow for long periods of the year exhibit seasonal camouflage: in winter they have a white coat, in summer a brown one.

The colors of fish and birds are much more vivid than those of mammals, for they derive from a wide range of specialized cells that produce different colors, the chromatophores. These are almost totally absent in mammals, which tend to be brown in color.

sense of smell, like us (microsmatics), or with none at all, like whales (anosmatics).

THE ADVENTURE OF COLOR

Even this characteristic can be attributed to the very long period spent by the oldest of the mammals in poorly lit surroundings. In fish, reptiles and birds the message conveyed by color is highly important and is left to special cells called chromatophores. Different colors require different types of cells: melanophores have a proteinic dark brown pigment, xanthophores a lipidic yellow pigment, erythrophores a red one and guanophores are responsible for iridescence. Color is of no importance in the dark and so mammals lost the genetic information to differentiate guanophores, xanthophores and erythrophores. The melanophores with their dark color remained, on the other hand, because a blackish silhouette is the best camouflage

in a dimly lit environment. To this day mammals that have clung to their nocturnal habits still have dark brown fur. But when the mammals began their expansion many orders changed their living habits and moved into diurnal and well-lit environments. In such circumstances a dark color no longer provided much camouflage and it would have been useful to return to more brightly colored forms. But the genetic information to synthesize the various types of chromatophore had been definitively lost: all that was available for evolution was the dark proteinic pigment of melanine. And so, through variations in the length of the melanine molecule, red, orange and yellow returned, although with much less brilliant results. On the whole, mammalian colors are dull rather than bright, but more than adequate to accomplish their task of allowing the animal to match its background enough to prey successfully or to protect itself from predators.

CAMOUFLAGE

Looking at a herd of zebra, with their striped coats, it is not immediately apparent that even this coloration has a mimetic value. By day the zebra is highly visible, but not particularly vulnerable because its eyes and sense of smell keep it constantly alert; at dusk or in dim light those black and white stripes break up the pattern of the animal, concealing it from predators. It is said that it is possible to come within 50 feet (15 meters) of a zebra at night without being aware of it.

5. EMBRYO AND SUCKLING

Of all animals, mammals have the slowest and most complex development, which is protracted long after birth, with mother and young bound together by close ties of nutrition and learning. This more or less prolonged relationship causes the high rate of intelligence manifested by the class as a whole.

DEVELOPMENT OF EMBRYO

Mammals are divided in three subclasses distinguished on the basis of their reproductive systems. Monotremes lay eggs like reptiles. Marsupials stay for a short time in the female's uterus and are born in a very undeveloped state and most growth takes place in mother's marsupium, or pouch. Placentals are carried in mother's womb for a longer period and are born in a completely developed form. During its development, through a placenta, the embryo draws from the mother's bloodstream all its nourishment and returns to it all its waste-product. This relationship, called gestation, may last from a few days to ten or more months, depending upon the speed of the embryo's development.

SUCKLING

The name "mammal" refers to the presence of mammary glands: in all mammal females, specialized glands develop which produce milk for suckling the young. They lie beneath the skin of the chest and open into teats, whose number depends upon the number of offspring to which the mother usually gives birth. Pigs for example have numerous pairs of teats that run from the armpit to the groin, so that as many as a dozen piglets can be suckled at a time. The females of many rodents also have a long row of mammary glands and give birth to numerous young. This is because such species are subject to heavy predation and have to make up for this high death rate by a rapid development in the uterus, by a large number of offspring and by a high rate of growth after

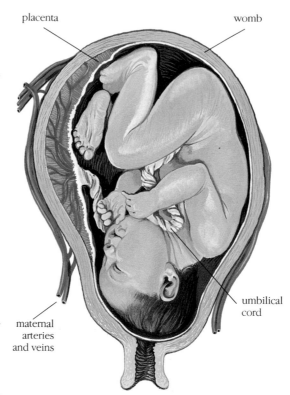

In placental mammals the embryo develops inside the mother's womb. Through the umbilical cord the placenta provides it with nourishment and eliminates its waste.

birth. When a species enjoys relative security, on the other hand, all these factors are reduced: development in mother's womb slows down (as among rhinoceroses, whose young are born after a gestation period of 15-16 months), the number of offspring falls as low as one and growth of the newborn animal is slow. This last feature is closely related to the quality of the milk.

MILK

The liquid secreted by the mammary glands, milk, contains all the substances needed for the growth of the young animal, which feeds solely on mother's milk for longer or shorter periods. As well as water, this liquid contains proteins and calcium required by the newborn animal to double its birthweight rapidly, fats used by the suckling both for body growth and as a source of energy, and milk sugar (lactose) which has an exclusively energetic function, being utilized for the metabolic needs of the organism. Milk also contains mineral salts, vitamins and hormones. Each species manufactures a milk, with a different composition of these substances, particularly suited to the growth patterns of its young. Rhinoceros' or human milk, for example, has a very high water content and a low protein content because in these mammals body growth is slow and the period of lactation is very long. In species whose young have to attain nutritional independence within a short period of time (e.g. the mouse), because of the heavy predation referred to above, the milk is very rich in organic substances, especially fats and proteins. The composition of milk also varies in relation to the environment in which the species live. In mammals adapted to survival in frosty climates, like polar bears, or living in the cold waters of the oceans, like whales, the fat content of milk is very high. Fats supply the calories needed to maintain body heat.

THE IMPORTANCE OF SUCKLING

Suckling establishes a relationship between mother and offspring that is important, not only because it satisfies the nutritional demands of the young animal, but also because it exerts a direct influence over mental development. We shall see in fact that intelligence, in our class, is based primarily on learning. And the newborn creature's first, and most important, teacher is its mother.

The word "mammal" refers to the fact that these animals have "mammary glands." In fact this class is distinguished from all others by the females' suckling of their young. The calf sucks milk for several months; the baby gorilla is nursed at its mother's breast until it is two years old.

Cow   Gorilla

10

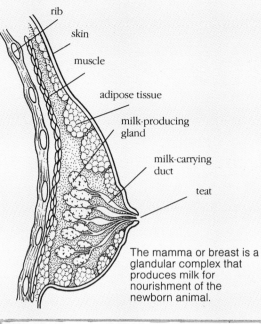

rib
skin
muscle
adipose tissue
milk-producing gland
milk-carrying duct
teat

The mamma or breast is a glandular complex that produces milk for nourishment of the newborn animal.

Mammals are divided into three large groups.

The **MONOTREMES** lay *eggs*, sit on them for about ten days and then suckle the young which are born at an incomplete stage of development.

The **MARSUPIALS** give birth to live young, in a very undeveloped state. Further growth and nourishment takes place in the mother's *marsupium* or pouch.

In **PLACENTALS** the entire development of the embryo takes place within the mother's womb, where it is nourished by means of the placenta. The young are usually born perfectly formed and are suckled at their mother's teats.

duck-billed platypus egg

newborn kangaroo

newborn leveret

The composition of mammalian milk varies from species to species and from place to place.

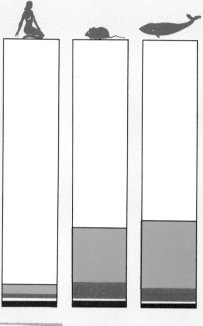

○ water
○ fats
○ proteins
○ lactose
● ashes

Indian rhinoceros

Left:
large-sized mammals have a very long period of gestation and lactation. The massive female of the great Indian rhinoceros bears a single calf after a gestation period of sixteen months. The newborn rhino weighs 140 pounds (65 kilos) and closely resembles the adult, lacking only the horn. During the first year of life it drinks 25 quarts (24 liters) of milk a day. It will not be weaned until it is two and a half years old.

Below:
the number of mammary glands varies in different species of mammals and depends on the number of young.

The young of the common opossum are born after a gestation period of 15 days. They are nursed in the pouch for 10 weeks, then emerge and cling to the mother's back.

Common opossum

Domestic pig

11

6. INTELLIGENCE, LEARNING, LIVING IN GROUPS

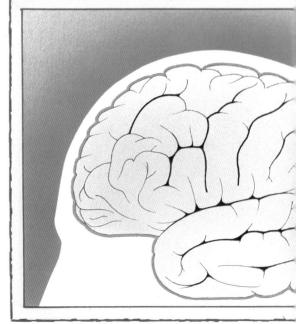

The human brain has a highly convoluted cerebral cortex (neocortex).

With mammals a new kind of behavior appears, or becomes more evident, in which actions as purely a matter of instinct in response to the environment are limited to a few cases. Intelligence has already been touched on in Chapter 16 of the *Dinosaurs and Birds* volume in this series: birds follow patterns of behavior often difficult to interpret, but which are far from what is generally regarded as intelligence. In mammals, although to varying degrees in the different orders, behavior appears to be much more complex and sophisticated.

A NEW AREA IN THE BRAIN

The new type of behavior is partly due to the presence of a new nervous area exclusive to mammals: the neocortex of the forebrain (telencephalon). Actually this area was already present in turtles (see the *Reptiles* volume in this series, Chapter 4), but it was small, and had only a scanty effect on the behavior of the animal. In mammals the neocortex controls all of the animal's nervous activity: information from sense organs are chaneled to this area, and from it depart commands for voluntary movement. But the neocortex has a crucial role in higher intellectual functions, the most important of which is learning; through the assimilation of new information and skills, the animal can continuously vary its patterns of behavior, according to changing circumstances and memorizing previous experiences.

THE CONVOLUTIONS

The extent of the neocortex is not the same in all mammals; in the most primitive, such as insectivores (see Chapter 15), it is confined to a dorsally located area, while in others it covers the whole brain; in still others it has grown to form many convolutions (the outer folds of the brain, also called "gray matter"). The larger the surface of the neocortex, the greater the number of nerve cells and the connections between them. There seems to be a relation between the extent of the neocortex and the quality of nervous activity, or the "intelligence" manifested by the animal in its behavior, but it is a generic one. Dolphins and whales, for example, have more convolutions in their brain than many apes or man himself, and yet they are much less intelligent. The origin and levels of intelligence cannot be explained on the basis of the size of nervous areas or the number of nerve cells, for they are linked to as yet unknown factors.

THE FIRST TEACHER

Thus the mammal appears at birth with a brain ready to learn and with a few actions and patterns of behavior already imprinted on its cells. From its mother the suckling begins to learn how to act and the rules of behavior. At the end of this phase, or contemporaneously with it, another period of training begins.

PLAY

The term play has connotations of futility, uselessness, and time wasted. In reality, play is the most important training for the young mammal. Play is not found in any other animals; neither fish nor reptiles nor birds have ever been seen playing with one another, that is, performing acts that have no definite purpose. In those animals the brain is already provided from birth with all the information necessary for hunting or avoiding being hunted. The mammal, on the other hand, learns through play all the skills necessary to live in its surroundings, and the patterns of behavior typical of its species. There are famous examples of the young of one species being adopted by animals of another and exhibiting, as adults, the behavior of their adoptive parents. There have even been cases of human children raised by wild mammals, who have acquired the same modes of behavior and of feeding as the animals with which they lived.

PERMANENT LEARNING

The process of training continues even after suckling has come to an end; the ability of the neocortex to assimilate new knowledge does not cease in the adult. Every experience is memorized as it may prove to be useful under similar conditions. The intelligence of the mammal is related to its readiness to adapt its behavior to changing circumstances.

LIVING IN GROUPS

Many mammals, especially predators, live in more or less numerous groups, and adopt patterns of behavior necessary to the survival of the group rather than to that of the individual. Thus among herbivores there are individuals that take on the responsibility of remaining alert for the safety of the herd, while some carnivores, the wolves for example, hunt in packs with tasks shared between the different members of the group. Intelligence is one of the mammals' trumpcards and has permitted their expansion and present dominion over the earth.

Lion

The close tie with the mother during the period of lactation, play with parents and with other animals of the same age and hunting in packs are all important factors in the development of the young animal's intelligence, based largely on learning. A number of examples are illustrated in these pages.
1) Two adult lions patiently look on as their cubs carry out feigned attacks.
2) A female gorilla dandling an adopted kitten.
3) A springbok suckling her young.
4) A female elephant seal protects her young from the furious battles between males.
5) An Indian elephant teaches her calf how to cool off in the river.
6) A wolf pack hunting a moose in deep snow.

12

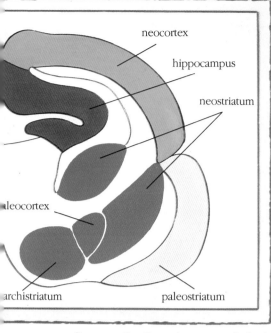

Cross-section through a mammal's brain, showing the new cerebral area of the neocortex.

neocortex

hippocampus

neostriatum

neocortex

archistriatum

paleostriatum

2

Gorilla

3

Springbok

1

4

Elephant seal

Indian elephant

6

Moose

Wolf

5

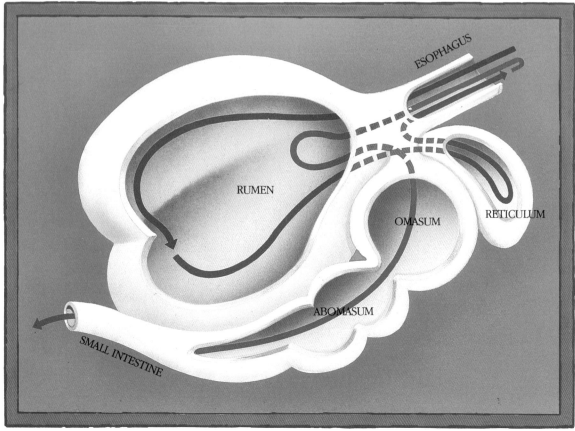

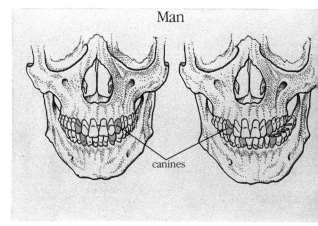

Ruminants have a stomach that is made up of four cavities. The fresh forage is accumulated in the first two, then it is regurgitated into the mouth (purple line). After thorough chewing, it is again swallowed and passed on to the other two (red line).

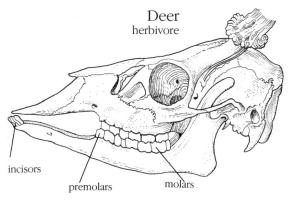

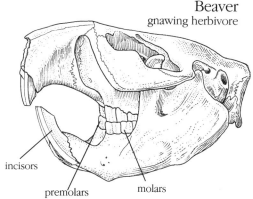

The canines allow vertical and lateral movements.

7. FEEDING

MASTICATION

The way in which mammals chew food and utilize it is another of their strong points, demonstrating the efficiency of their evolution and explaining their broad diffusion. Among extinct reptiles, the gigantic herbivorous dinosaurs had a highly specialized and functional digestive apparatus. Living reptiles have very slow digestion, since they lack any means of chewing and they swallow the prey as a whole. In the *Dinosaurs and Birds* volume in this series (Chapter 13) we saw how birds, which have no teeth, solved the problem of efficient food utilization by chewing with the stomach.

Homeothermy, a typical mammalian feature, demands, as pointed out in Chapter 2, a continual consumption of energy. This means that the mammal must not only eat a great deal, but also speed up

digestion in order to provide the organism with an adequate supply, without any long breaks, of organic substances to convert into heat. By mastication, solid lumps of food are broken up into small particles. Dentition varying greatly in number and shape is one of the distinctive features of mammals. Instead of the conical tooth, typical of other vertebrates, mammals have the incisors for grazing or piercing, the canines for tearing and the premolars and molars for grinding the food. Mastication normally involves a side-to-side movement of the lower jaw, but this is not an inflexible rule: in rodents for example the movement is from front to back, while in other orders it is almost rotary. The type of food preferred by each species (whether herbivorous, carnivorous or omnivorous) has also molded the shape of teeth used in mastication to make them more efficient.

The digestion process breaks down food into

simple molecules (sugars, fats, proteins) capable of being absorbed into the body of the animal. Alone among the vertebrates, mammals begin digesting food while it is still in the mouth. Mammalian saliva, formed by the salivary glands, not only helps to convert food to a moistened paste which can be easily swallowed, but also begins chemical transformation of eaten substances, thanks to the action of a digestive enzyme, ptyalin, that breaks down starches into sugars.

THE HERBIVOROUS DIET

Plants represent an abundant and sure source of food for animals: they are present wherever environmental conditions permit; they are easy prey, which does not run away and can at best defend itself with spines, thorns or poisons. They do however present a

14

To obtain their food, carnivores that hunt in packs even attack prey larger than themselves. Once they have detected the presence of a wildebeest with their powerful smell, African wild dogs will pursue it for miles and miles. Seven times out of ten, these long and exhausting chases end in the death of the big herbivore.

Wildebeest

Wild dog

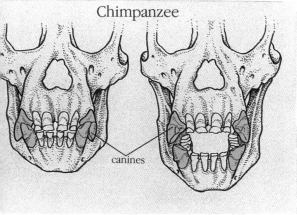

Chimpanzee

canines

The canines prevent sideways movement.

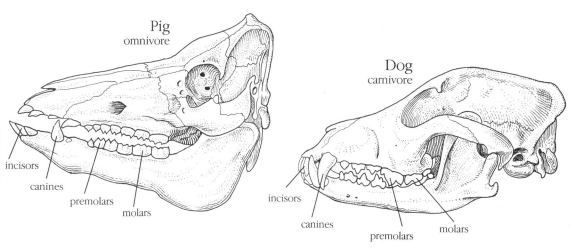

Pig
omnivore

incisors

canines

premolars

molars

Dog
carnivore

incisors

canines

premolars

molars

The dentition with incisors, canines, premolars and molars is a typical feature of mammals. It has evolved in different forms in accordance with the animal's diet, as is shown in these two pages.

problem as far as digestion is concerned. No vertebrate possesses the enzymes required to carry out this process, which means that vegetable food would pass through the alimentary canal intact. In order to exploit this important and economical energy source, herbivores avail themselves of the assistance of micro-organisms. In the stomach and intestines of these mammals lives a population of protozoans and bacteria capable of breaking down cellulose (the most important component of plant matter) into simpler molecules that can be more easily assailed by digestive juices. In this way a sort of symbiosis is established between the animal and the micro-organisms: the former assimilates the vegetable matter thanks to the activity of the latter, while the latter, living on the same food, are able to grow and reproduce. In spite of this indispensable aid, the breakdown of cellulose remains a difficult and slow process. To assist it, some herbivores have adopted other strategies.

RUMINATION

Herbivorous mammals with the capacity to ruminate, such as common cattle, have a four-chambered stomach. When grazing, a cow tears up grass or leaves that are partially chewed, rapidly swallowed and stored in the first and most voluminous chamber of the stomach, the *rumen*. Later, perhaps when the animal lies down in a place safe from predators, rumination begins. The food passes from the rumen to the second chamber of the stomach, the *reticulum*. From there it is regurgitated, in small fragments, into the mouth for further mastication and mixed thoroughly with the saliva for a long time. When it is moved to a cud, or food bolus, the vegetable matter is swallowed once again and passes through the *omasum*, the third chamber of the stomach, where water is absorbed, and then to the *abomasum*, the fourth chamber where proper digestion begins.

HERBIVORES' INTESTINE

Since the cellulose molecule is broken down slowly, the intestine of an herbivore is very long, allowing the food to remain there for a long time before completing its passage. Herbivores also possess a blind section of the intestine where the absorption of cellulose molecules (glucosium) is carried out more thoroughly.

CARNIVORES' FEEDING

Meat is far easier to digest than grass and requires teeth suited for tearing the food rather than grinding it. In fact the teeth of herbivores tend to be flat, while those of carnivores are provided with sharp crests, like pointed canines and scissor-like molars, to tear the meat of the prey into pieces.

8. MOVEMENT

LIMBS AND GIRDLES IN AMPHIBIANS AND REPTILES

In the history of vertebrates the limbs have evolved from the fins of the crossopterygian fish and the way they are jointed with the pelvic and pectoral girdles reveals this origin (see the *Amphibians* volume in this series, Chapter 8). In amphibians and reptiles the limb is set sideways with respect to the body; the humerus in the forelimb and the femur in the hind limb protrude laterally, while the remaining bones are set perpendicularly to the humerus or femur in order to reach the ground. This type of joint does not permit motion to be either agile or fast, since it involves moving only one limb at a time: for example, the right forelimb first, which the left hind limb follows, then the left forelimb and finally the right hind limb.

HOW THE DINOSAURS RAN

This large group of reptiles which dominated the whole Mesozoic Era had discovered that motion could be speeded up by using the hind limbs alone. This discovery brought immediate rewards: many species of dinosaurs appeared with a bipedal gait and very robust hind limbs capable of considerable speed. This development was a major factor in the dinosaurs' long domination of the other reptiles: increased speed meant both more efficient hunting and better chances of evading predators. However erect posture among reptiles was limited to the dinosaurs alone.

LIMBS AND GIRDLES IN THE MAMMALS

The real novelty in our own class was the new relation between the limbs and the pelvic and pectoral girdles: the limbs are no longer set sideways on to the body, but are underneath it, like four pillars fitting snugly into the bones of the girdle. Thus the limbs move in a single plane like a pendulum and are lifted in pairs; further the spinal column remains rigid while the animal walks. This change met with immediate success as well. Many orders of mammals have specialized in running and are remarkably fast, even though champions like the cheetah, able to reach 70 miles (112 kilometers) per hour, can only maintain such top speeds for less than a minute.

REDUCTION OF CONTACT WITH THE GROUND

The evolution of a limb suited to running involves a profound modification of the way in which it makes contact with the ground. Normally the limb is supported by the entire hand (or foot), but in carnivores the hand (or foot) is raised so that only the finger, or toe, rests on the ground. In the ungulates which, while they hold no records, are capable of maintaining considerable speeds for long periods, contact with the ground has been further reduced so that the animal runs on the tips of its toes, or of a single toe, as in the case of the horse. In these animals, the nail or hoof is very sturdy and thick, for it bears the weight of the body and sustains the thrust in running.

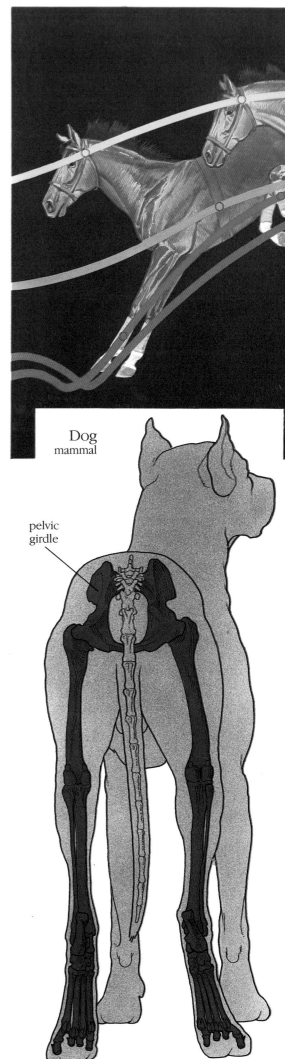

Dog
mammal

pelvic girdle

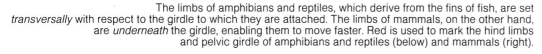

The limbs of amphibians and reptiles, which derive from the fins of fish, are set *transversally* with respect to the girdle to which they are attached. The limbs of mammals, on the other hand, are *underneath* the girdle, enabling them to move faster. Red is used to mark the hind limbs and pelvic girdle of amphibians and reptiles (below) and mammals (right).

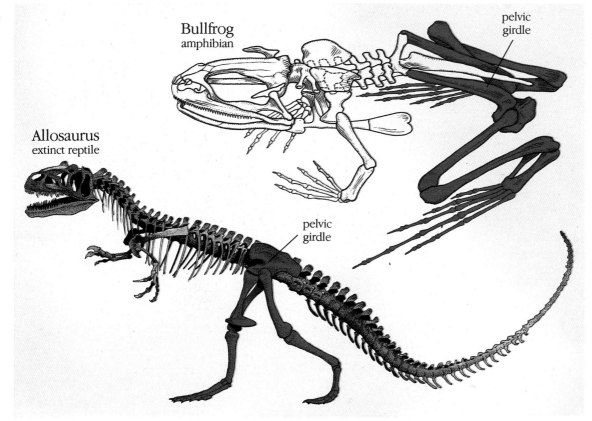

Bullfrog
amphibian

pelvic girdle

Allosaurus
extinct reptile

pelvic girdle

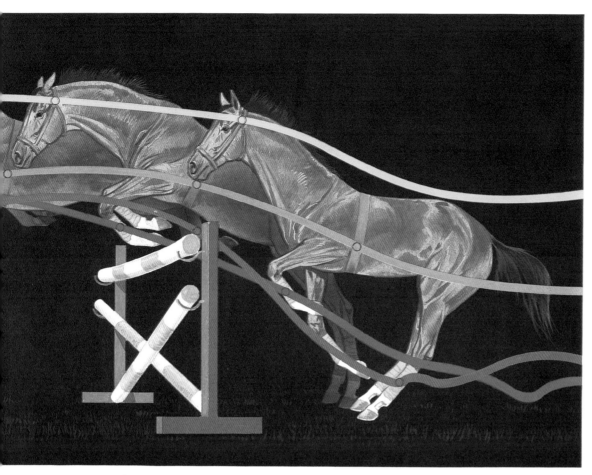

HOPPING AS A WAY OF MOVING

A few mammals have adopted a bipedal gait, but one in which both feet move forward together so that the animal hops. This is the typical gait of the kangaroo, a highly evolved marsupial that at top speed is as fast as a racehorse and covers about 10 feet (3 meters) at a bound. Moving by leaps, the body leans forward, making a heavy tail necessary to balance its weight. The same thing was true of the bipedal dinosaurs.

NO MAMMAL CRAWLS

Crawling is a way of moving used by both amphibians and reptiles. It presents considerable advantages and allows precise ecological niches to be occupied. In spite of this no mammal, neither past nor present, has ever crawled; all move over the ground on the customary legs. This difference may be due to the fact that while amphibians and reptiles move, their spinal column has marked snake-like twistings (that are the basis of the crawling movement), whereas the spinal column of mammals remains essentially steady and rigid.

When running, and even when walking, all mammals, such as the horse (left) and the lion (below) move their limbs in a single plane, although they are also able to move them sideways.

Horse

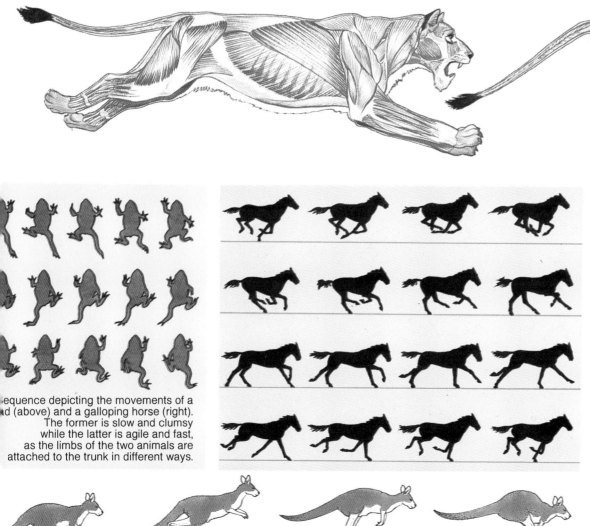

Lioness

...equence depicting the movements of a ...d (above) and a galloping horse (right). The former is slow and clumsy while the latter is agile and fast, as the limbs of the two animals are attached to the trunk in different ways.

The kangaroo moves at speed by hopping on its two rear limbs.

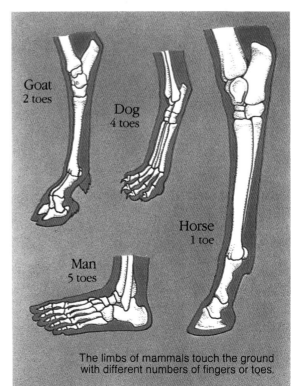

Goat
2 toes

Dog
4 toes

Horse
1 toe

Man
5 toes

The limbs of mammals touch the ground with different numbers of fingers or toes.

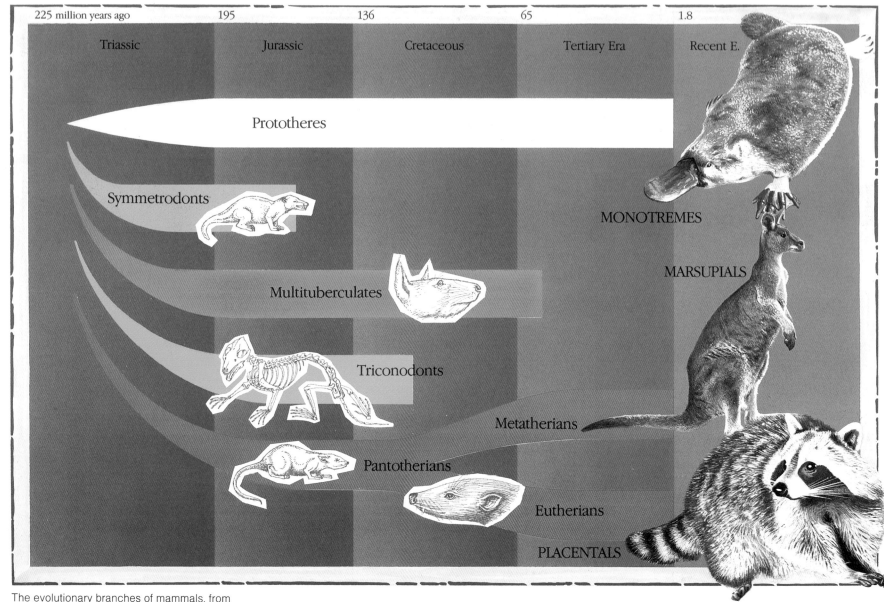

The evolutionary branches of mammals, from the Secondary Era to the Recent Era.

Timeline labels: 225 million years ago | 195 | 136 | 65 | 1.8

Era labels: Triassic | Jurassic | Cretaceous | Tertiary Era | Recent E.

Branch labels: Prototheres, Symmetrodonts, Multituberculates, Triconodonts, Pantotherians, Metatherians, Eutherians

Group labels: MONOTREMES, MARSUPIALS, PLACENTALS

9. THE EVOLUTIONARY BRANCHES OF MAMMALS

In Chapter 1 we saw the strong tendency of an evolutionary line of the therapsid reptiles, the theriodonts, to acquire mammalian features. The theriodonts are perfect intermediate forms between reptiles and mammals. However, true mammals probably appeared much later, during the Jurassic Period, some 180 million years ago, but the dating remains uncertain, owing to the scarcity of fossil remains. The first mammals were small in size and had fragile bones, making it particularly difficult and unlikely for the skeleton to undergo fossilization. Today skull fragments, jaws with teeth and a few other bones are all that remain of those animals.

THE TOOTH

The form of the mammalian tooth has always been carefully studied since it is one of the main features of the class. Mastication which, as we have already seen, is peculiar to mammals, imposes a special type of teeth and jaw. From examination of the fossil remains of mammals living with dinosaurs in the Jurassic Period, it can be deduced that there were at least five evolutionary branches of the new class whose habits and skeletal structures already differed. There is still

some doubt as to whether these five evolutionary lines had a common origin or had developed independently.

THE PROTOTHERES

These extinct mammals still had many features typical of reptiles. The prototheres were never widespread and their descendants, the monotremes (see Chapter 11), have survived, thanks to a lack of competition with other forms, in the isolated areas of Australia and New Guinea.

THE TRICONODONTS

This extinct branch of primitive mammals was made up of small and slight forms, similar to a rat; only the *Triconodon* attained the size of a cat. Their common feature was their teeth, usually numerous, each one bearing three pointed cones (hence the name). Insects or small animals probably represented their main source of food. The triconodonts became extinct early on, during the Cretaceous Period, without leaving any descendants.

THE MULTITUBERCULATES

This evolutionary branch also failed to survive to the present day, but it became extinct much more recently, in the middle of the Tertiary Era. The name refers to the highly specialized dentition of these mammals. They had well-developed incisors, perhaps adapted to gnawing or tearing off pieces of bark, which would then be finely ground by the premolars, sometimes exceptionally broad and provided with transverse crests. The multituberculates probably chewed with a front-to-back movement of the lower jaw, rather than a side-to-side one. Despite their high degree of specialization, all the multituberculates vanished some 50 million years ago.

THE SYMMETRODONTS

These were small animals which grew no larger than a mouse, with teeth typical of the carnivores or insectivores. Each tooth had a central pointed cone preceded and succeeded by two smaller and symmetrical cones, hence the name. The symmetrodonts were not very successful and

18

PLACENTALS

Carnivores · Artiodactyls · Cetaceans · Perissodactyls · Hyracoids · Proboscideans · Rodents · Primates · Lagomorphs · Pholidota · Sirenians · Insectivores · Tubulidentates · Chiropters · Dermopters · Edentates

Evolutionary diffusion of placental mammals that took place at the height of the Tertiary Era.

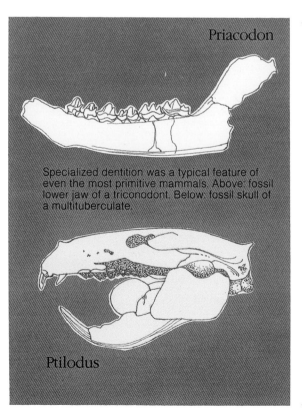

Priacodon

Ptilodus

Specialized dentition was a typical feature of even the most primitive mammals. Above: fossil lower jaw of a triconodont. Below: fossil skull of a multituberculate.

Triconodon

One of the most primitive mammals alive during the Jurassic Period, the *Triconodon* was the size of a rat and had a body covered with fur.

disappeared very early, during the Jurassic Period, leaving no living descendants.

THE PANTOTHERIANS

From these evolved the most successful evolutionary branch. Before their extinction, during the Cretaceous Period, the pantotherians gave rise to two other groups, both extinct, but destined to be the ancestors of all living mammals, excluding the monotremes. From the metatherians was derived the evolutionary line of the marsupials (see Chapters 12 and 13) and from the eutherians the line of the placentals, so rich in orders that we are reproducing it in the above diagram.

Little is known about the ancient pantotherians, but their features were probably the same as those mentioned for other branches: small size, nocturnal habits, insects as a source of nutrition.

19

10. THE UNSETTLED HISTORY OF MAMMALS

Today mammals have a precise and apparently stable distribution, which is the outcome of a troubled period in which massive migrations occurred and a number of major orders appeared or disappeared.

AN EXPLOSIVE EVOLUTION

The evolutionary branch of the placental mammals, derived from the pantotherians, appeared during the Cretaceous Period, probably in Asia. The early placentals were small insectivorous animals with nocturnal habits like their predecessors. But after the extinction of the dinosaurs, a variety of evolutionary branches began to emerge from these insignificant insectivores, each specialized for the colonization of a particular habitat. After less than 10 million years, an incredibly short time from the perspective of the evolutionary process, not only had all the orders living today appeared, but also many other species which have not survived to our own times.

A FANTASTIC WORLD

The earth was already firmly in the grip of the mammals during the Tertiary Era. The birds, which had tried to take the place of the dinosaurs, had been driven back into their natural environment, the air. Yet an explorer traveling the continents of that age would have encountered animals that were either completely different from modern mammals or that had only a vague resemblance to them. Before attaining forms similar to those with which we are familiar and settling into the geographic areas in which they are found today, the mammals had to pass through a long period of modifications, migrations and reshufflings of species, brought about by the movement of continental masses and consequent changes in the environment.

CONTINENTAL DRIFT

During the Mesozoic Era the lands above sea-level, which originally formed a single block that then broke up into two large continents, assumed the form that they have today after a series of orogenetic shifts. The continually moving landmasses have at times joined up again, making possible the movement of fauna from one part to another, and at other times have definitively drawn apart.

At the time that Australia broke away, for example, it was populated solely by marsupials. When the placentals began their expansion, it was no longer possible for them to reach this part of the world. Antarctica was also isolated along with its cargo of marsupials, but its southward drift and the blanket of ice that resulted made life impossible for its passengers, which all became extinct. The two Americas were isolated, each with its characteristic population of mammals, but were then briefly reunited about 60 million years ago, allowing passage of the edentates from south to north. The two continents then separated again, only to be reconnected finally 10 million years ago, with a new mixing of species. Some, like the llama, migrated from north to south, while others, like the three-toed sloth, moved in the opposite direction.

Megatherium

The *Megatherium*, which lived in South America during the Pleistocene Period, was a gigantic placental mammal. It was the ancestor of the modern sloths and was 20-23 feet (6-7 meters) long.

THE LINK BETWEEN AMERICA AND EUROPE

Numerous transfers have taken place from one continent to the other, thanks to the link provided, at least in periods when the climate was favorable, by what is today the Bering Strait. The horse, for instance, emerged in America, from where a few members of the *Hipparion* species migrated to Europe 10-12 million years ago. While these continued to evolve, the American species died out. The Americas did not see the horse again until it was brought back by man. The camel followed the same route, whereas the mammoth and the bison moved in the opposite direction. In spite of its high latitude, the land-bridge between America and Europe must have been covered by dense tropical forests and vegetation at the beginning of the Eocene Period. It was also traversed by the earliest species of primates, which lived in only that kind of habitat. The *Plesiadapis* (see Chapter 23), for example, was very common in both continents. But with the disappearance of forests later in the Eocene Period, the possibility of transit by primates was removed and the isolated populations continued their evolution separately, developing different forms.

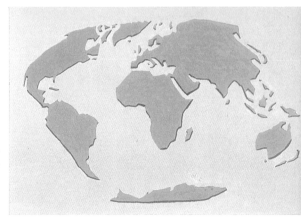

TODAY.

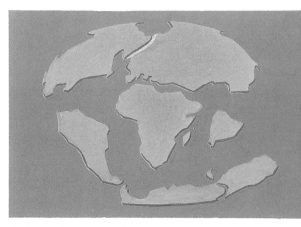

BEGINNING OF THE TERTIARY ERA, 65 MILLION YEARS AGO.

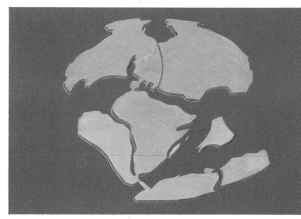

CRETACEOUS PERIOD, ABOUT 135 MILLION YEARS AGO.

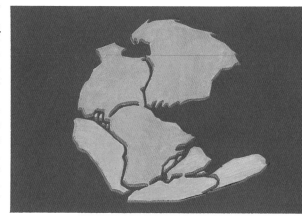

TRIASSIC PERIOD, ABOUT 200 MILLION YEARS AGO.

The four maps represent reconstructions of some of the various positions assumed by the continents in different geological eras, before reaching their present ones.

20

Illustrated here are reconstructions of placental mammals that lived in different periods and places, all of them herbivores and large in size.

THE *UINTATHERIUM*, BELONGING TO THE EXTINCT ORDER OF THE AMBLYPODS, LIVED IN NORTH AMERICA DURING THE EOCENE PERIOD (SEE CH. 19 AS WELL). TWELVE FEET (3.5 METERS) LONG, IT RESEMBLED A RHINOCEROS AND HAD THREE PAIRS OF BONY PROTUBERANCES ON ITS SKULL AND HIGHLY DEVELOPED UPPER CANINES.

RELATED TO THE MODERN CAMELS, THE *ALTICAMELUS* WAS AN ARTIODACTYL UNGULATE THAT INHABITED NORTH AMERICA DURING THE PLIOCENE PERIOD. TWELVE FEET (3.5 METERS) TALL, IT BROWSED ON THE LEAVES OF TREES.

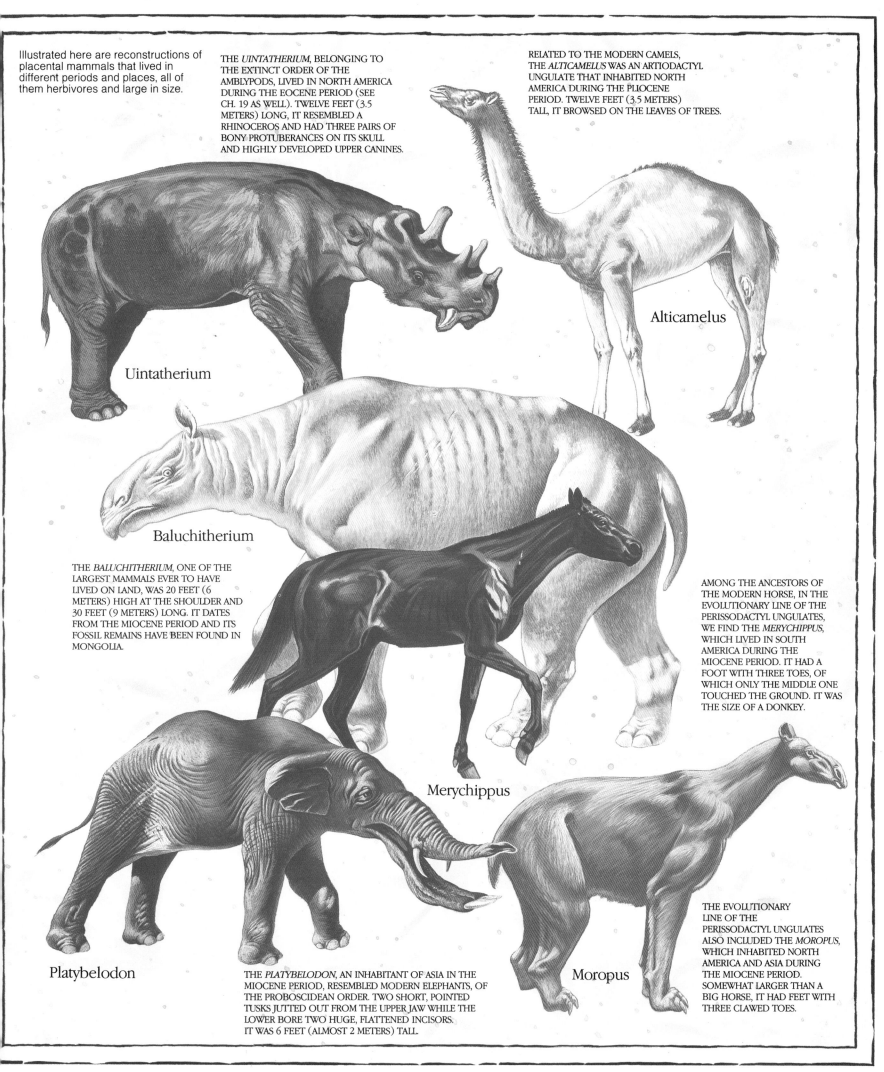

Alticamelus

Uintatherium

Baluchitherium

THE *BALUCHITHERIUM*, ONE OF THE LARGEST MAMMALS EVER TO HAVE LIVED ON LAND, WAS 20 FEET (6 METERS) HIGH AT THE SHOULDER AND 30 FEET (9 METERS) LONG. IT DATES FROM THE MIOCENE PERIOD AND ITS FOSSIL REMAINS HAVE BEEN FOUND IN MONGOLIA.

AMONG THE ANCESTORS OF THE MODERN HORSE, IN THE EVOLUTIONARY LINE OF THE PERISSODACTYL UNGULATES, WE FIND THE *MERYCHIPPUS*, WHICH LIVED IN SOUTH AMERICA DURING THE MIOCENE PERIOD. IT HAD A FOOT WITH THREE TOES, OF WHICH ONLY THE MIDDLE ONE TOUCHED THE GROUND. IT WAS THE SIZE OF A DONKEY.

Merychippus

Platybelodon

THE *PLATYBELODON*, AN INHABITANT OF ASIA IN THE MIOCENE PERIOD, RESEMBLED MODERN ELEPHANTS, OF THE PROBOSCIDEAN ORDER. TWO SHORT, POINTED TUSKS JUTTED OUT FROM THE UPPER JAW WHILE THE LOWER BORE TWO HUGE, FLATTENED INCISORS. IT WAS 6 FEET (ALMOST 2 METERS) TALL.

Moropus

THE EVOLUTIONARY LINE OF THE PERISSODACTYL UNGULATES ALSO INCLUDED THE *MOROPUS*, WHICH INHABITED NORTH AMERICA AND ASIA DURING THE MIOCENE PERIOD. SOMEWHAT LARGER THAN A BIG HORSE, IT HAD FEET WITH THREE CLAWED TOES.

Duck-billed platypus

New Guinea
Australia
Tasmania

The duck-billed platypus lives on the banks of streams and rivers in Australia and Tasmania. It has a streamlined body about 20 inches (50 centimeters) long and spends most of the time underwater searching for snails, crayfish, worms and insect larvae with its highly sensitive bill. It can remain submerged for up to five minutes. Inset: distribution of the monotremes.

The duck-billed platypus also swims on the surface of the water without making any noise.

To clean its glossy coat, the duck-billed platypus uses its bill in exactly the way that birds do.

When on dry land, the duck-billed platypus often remains motionless with its body in an upright posture, resting on its hind limbs.

Immediately after hatching, the newborn platypuses climb onto their mother's belly and lick the milk that oozes from the mammary glands along small tufts of fur; in fact the female has no teats.

11. MONOTREMES

Representing the only surviving order of the evolutionary line of the prototheres, these unusual animals are of extremely ancient origin. They may belong to a branch of mammals completely independent of the others, derived directly from the synapsid reptiles of the Triassic Period. They are found in Australia, New Guinea and Tasmania, which they have never left and where they have never undergone much development. One still often comes across the statement, even in school texts, that monotremes represent a link between reptiles and mammals, or even between birds and mammals; hence it is worth emphasizing that they are an independent evolutionary branch of the mammals. They may or may not be of autonomous origin, but in any case they are very remote from the ones to which other more familiar mammals belong.

REPTILIAN CHARACTERISTICS

The monotremes are the only mammals that lay eggs, from which emerge embryos that develop in a very similar way to those of reptiles. Their skeleton has many bones typical of reptiles, especially in the thoracic cage and the pectoral and pelvic girdles. Teeth are present at birth, but are soon replaced by a duck-like horny bill.

MAMMALIAN CHARACTERISTICS

That the monotremes belong to our own class is clearly demonstrated not only by the bones of their skull, but by the presence on their body of fur and diffuse mammary glands. Monotremes have a very dense coat of long and fine fur. Their mammalian glands are very primitive and more closely resemble sweat-glands. Since there are no teats, the milk (which does not contain lactose, the sugar present in the milk of all other mammals) oozes from small tufts of hair that are licked by the newborn animal.

THE DUCK-BILLED PLATYPUS

In 1798 the skin of a duck-billed platypus, complete with head, arrived in Europe for the first time. The scientists that examined it found absurd the presence of a duck's bill in an animal covered with fur. In those days sailing ships returning from the Indian Ocean often brought strange creatures, fabricated from bits of different animals with the aid of glue and thread, to sell them as exotic curiosities. So this first specimen was considered a fraud by European scientists. Many years went by and it was not until a living platypus was brought to Europe that it was recognized as a real animal. Closer studies revealed that this bizarre creature had many odd characteristics, incongruous for a mammal: a broad snout resembling the bill of a duck, webbed feet like amphibians or aquatic birds, venom glands and—in an even more astonishing departure from mammalian norm—egg-laying females, like reptiles.

Platypuses are uniquely adapted for a wholly

22

Zaglossus

Tasmanian echidna

Short-nosed echidna

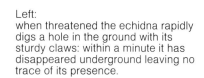

The female of the echidna or spiny anteater incubates her single soft-shelled egg in a temporary pouch that develops on her belly during the breeding season.

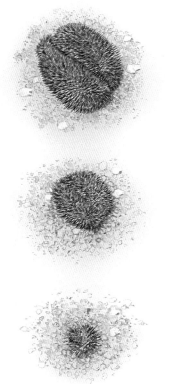

Left:
when threatened the echidna rapidly digs a hole in the ground with its sturdy claws: within a minute it has disappeared underground leaving no trace of its presence.

The *Zaglossus* and the echidna live in Australia, Tasmania and New Guinea. They are nocturnal animals similar to porcupines, with a dense coat of bristles and an array of long, pale spines on the back. They feed on ants and when they come upon a nest, they open it with their forelegs and gather up the insects with a long and slender tongue that darts out from the end of the tubular snout.

aquatic life. In addition to having webbed feet, their body is streamlined, their flattened tail is powerful in swimming, and they can stay underwater for two minutes. They feed on freshwater crustaceans, fish, insects and larvae, rooting trough the muddy bottoms of Australian lakes, ponds and streams with their pliable and highly sensitive snout. At birth the duck-billed platypus has a mouth with 34 teeth, but these are gradually lost until they are completely replaced by the horny bill. The males are one of the very few venomous mammals: each hind foot carries a spur, with a gland that secretes poison, which can wound man and cause weeks of suffering. Platypuses adapt to a wide range of living conditions, and they can reproduce even in captivity. The females lay from one to three eggs in concealed nests of leaves and incubate them for ten days deep within the banks of rivers which hold their burrows. The young are blind and naked when they hatch and remain in the nests for four months.

THE ECHIDNA

This animal, living in Australia and New Guinea, is also known as the "spiny anteater" since it feeds on ants and termites that it plucks up with its long, sticky, snake-like tongue. The long, tubular snout, reinforced by a horny case, is also capable of poking into crevices, rotten logs and nests in search of insects. Echidnas have no teeth, but the palate is lined with a horny substance that enables the food to be triturated. There are two species of echidnas, both with a covering of spines, which usually project through the fur, resembling porcupines' and hedgehogs' quills. When disturbed the echidna, a mainly nocturnal animal, rolls up into a ball, because spines are its only means of defense.

23

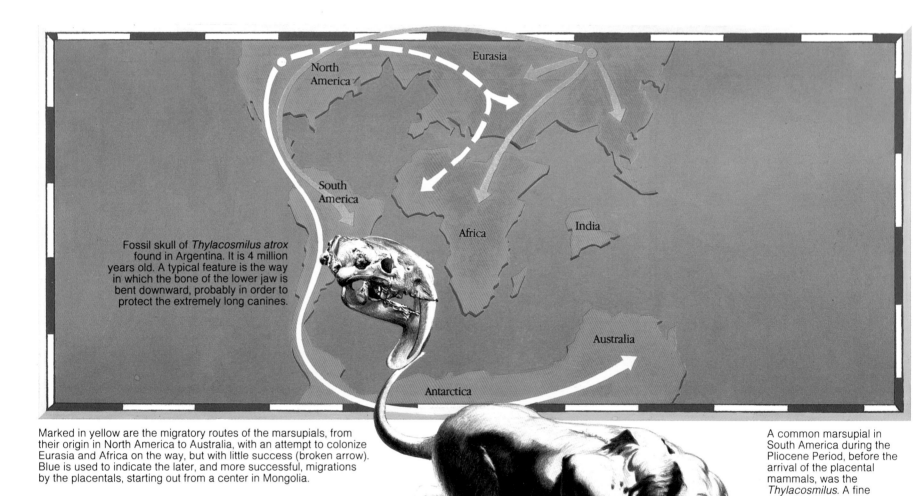

Fossil skull of *Thylacosmilus atrox* found in Argentina. It is 4 million years old. A typical feature is the way in which the bone of the lower jaw is bent downward, probably in order to protect the extremely long canines.

Marked in yellow are the migratory routes of the marsupials, from their origin in North America to Australia, with an attempt to colonize Eurasia and Africa on the way, but with little success (broken arrow). Blue is used to indicate the later, and more successful, migrations by the placentals, starting out from a center in Mongolia.

A common marsupial in South America during the Pliocene Period, before the arrival of the placental mammals, was the *Thylacosmilus*. A fine example of convergence due to a similarity in feeding habits, it closely resembled the *Smilodon* (a placental carnivore also extinct) in appearance, size and the extremely long and curved upper canines.

Thylacosmilus

12. AMERICAN MARSUPIALS

The first evolutionary line originated from the pantotherians were the marsupials, a group of mammals which still exists. They owe their name to a pouch in the female's skin—known as the marsupium—opening to the front in some, to the rear in others, and missing in a few species of the order. In it the young, born at a very undeveloped stage, are allowed to complete their growth in safety.

The story of this branch of modern mammals is particularly interesting, filled with hectic events and mysteries. The first marsupials appeared in North America in the middle of the Cretaceous Period, about 130 million years ago, quickly asserting themselves over other mammals. They were however unable to compete with the dinosaurs, which ruled all over the earth at the time.

A BIBLICAL MIGRATION

From North America the marsupials started on an impressive migration. First they invaded and colonized South America, then Antarctica and finally Australia. This move was possible because at that time all those landmasses were connected as shown in the map above. However, since not all geologists accept this hypothesis, other explanations could be advanced for the appearance of marsupials at different times in those continents. In any case, after occupation by the marsupials, Antarctica and Australia split off from South America (or from South Africa?) and separated from one another to move off in

different directions. Antarctica headed south, where its climate became increasingly cold, to the point of causing the extinction of all living creatures. Australia traveled eastwards—a direction in which it is still moving at the respectable speed of 2 inches (5 centimeters) per year—and so its population of marsupials was able to continue its evolution.

The marsupials also moved from North America into Europe and Africa, but did not meet with much success, to judge by the scarcity of fossil remains of ancient marsupials found in these two continents.

DIFFICULTIES COMMENCE

But towards the end of the Cretaceous Period, in Asia, the pantotherians gave rise to the evolutionary line of the placental mammals, characterized by a long development of the embryo inside the uterus. These new mammals asserted themselves rapidly and began to expand in every direction. Their spread made life difficult for the marsupials, which in fact died out in Europe, Africa and North America, while they managed to work out a mode of coexistence in South America.

THE AMERICAN MARSUPIALS

In the period between the extinction of the dinosaurs and the arrival of the placentals, the marsupials had occupied every ecological niche available in the Americas. Both herbivorous and carnivorous forms evolved; among the latter it is worth mentioning the

Probable expansion of marsupials into the different continents, in relation to geological periods.

	Australia	South America	North America	Europe	Asia Afric
Holocene					
Pleistocene					
Pliocene					
Miocene					
Oligocene					
Eocene					
Paleocene					
Upper Cretaceous					
Lower Cretaceous					
Jurassic					

24

Buzzard

Virginia opossum

Mouse opossum

Yapok

Of living American marsupials three are illustrated here that belong to the *Didelphidae* family. A Virginia opossum defends her young from a buzzard that has suddenly dropped from the sky, baring her teeth and hissing; she is backed up by the most courageous of her offspring. Angry opossums are very dangerous and their mouths bristling with teeth can be opened to an angle of 180 degrees. When they can see no other way out, they play dead. The mouse opossum has large membranous ears and very keen hearing. It is a nocturnal marsupial that lives in the trees, leaping from trunk to trunk with great agility. The yapok lives on the banks of streams and pools. When diving, the female is able to tightly close the rear opening of the pouch, so that her young do not get wet. The long tactile whiskers on the muzzle are used to find prey underwater.

extinct *Thylacosmilus,* with its very long canines closely resembling those of the placental *Smilodon* (see Chapter 20). The success of the placental mammals had a devastating effect on the marsupials: those still to be found in America today can be regarded as the last survivors of a once great empire.

THE OPOSSUMS

After the kangaroos, the opossums are the most familiar of the marsupials. They live in Central and South America, where they originated, and also in North America, where they emigrated when the two continents were joined up again, about 10 million years ago. The opossums belong to the *Didelphidae* family, the most primitive of all living marsupials. They are distinguished by their thick and soft fur coats, which are so highly sought after and appreciated, that the animals are also bred commercially. They are generally nocturnal and predominantly carnivorous, although remarkably adapted to a wide range of

feeding habits. As soon as they are born, the young of most species, ill-prepared for life independent of their mother's body, find their way to the marsupium, where they can suck milk from the teats, and where they have shelter, warmth and food for two months.

VIRGINIA OPOSSUM

Also known as the true opossum, *Didelphis virginiana* is the most typical of its family. It is distinguished by its fur of long and shaggy tufts of hair. It is the only marsupial that has extended its range into the heart of North American woods, where it moves around at night, hunting for any living, dead or putrefying animal. These feeding habits may be the basis for its repellent body odor, which represents an excellent means of defense against most carnivores. This species is much feared by farmers because of its reputed liking for domestic poultry. Opossums have a very short life-span, no longer than two years in general, and therefore reproduce very rapidly.

MOUSE OPOSSUM

This small animal (*Marmosa*) lives in Central and South America. It has no pouch and carries its young on its back until they are about three months old. Like most opossums, it uses its long, prehensile tail for support when moving through the branches of trees in search of fruits and insects. It is distinguished by its short and wooly fur.

YAPOK

This species of opossum (*Chironectes minimus*), also called water opossum, lives in South America, has a pouch that opens to the rear, webbed hind feet and a preference for the water and damp habitats. It is a nocturnal hunter of aquatic insects, fish, amphibians and all that lives and can be caught in the water. The yapok is at ease in the water and resembles the otter, but has a more timid and less playful character.

13. AUSTRALIAN MARSUPIALS

Fossil skull of *Diprotodon*, a marsupial found in pleistocenic layers in Australia.

On the Australian continent were and are present all the principal ecological niches found on earth: deserts, savannas, grasslands, mountains, forests and so on. Ever since this enormous mass was detached from the other continents, the marsupials have had a much longer time to evolve and adapt to the different habitats than the placental mammals, yet they have not developed to the same degree.

EVOLUTIONARY VIGOR

This characteristic of living creatures is difficult to define and quantify, but it can be described in a few words as the capacity of a major evolutionary line to form many different families or genuses, and exploit every possible food source. For example, in the upper Cretaceous Period there were 9 genuses of marsupials and 10 million years later there were still 9; over the same span of time the number of genuses among the placentals went up from 8 to 80. Evolutionary vigor seems to take place at a different pace in different orders.

CONVERGENCE

Convergence, one of the most impressive phenomena of evolution, becomes evident when studying Australia's different marsupial fauna. The same environment and the same food range produce—in quite unrelated evolutionary lines—equivalent or identical shapes or functions. Thus many Australian marsupials have differentiated along lines clearly parallel to those taken by the higher placental mammals living in most parts of the world. Equivalents can be found to placental wolves, such as the Tasmanian wolf, today reduced to a handful of animals in the mountains of Tasmania. There are equivalents to weasels and raccoons, such as the tiger cat; to bears, like the koala; to flying squirrels, such as the gliding petaurus; to mice and rats, such as the musky rat kangaroo; to dormice, such as the pygmy possum; and to anteaters, such as the numbat.

THE KANGAROO

Worthy of special attention is the kangaroo, which symbolizes the marsupial fauna of Australia. It is not a very primitive mammal, since its origin dates back to 10-15 million years ago. The kangaroos are browsers and grazers, playing the role that four-footed herbivores assume elsewhere. There are no horses, zebras, wildebeest, or antelopes in Australia, because their ideal habitat is firmly in the grip of the kangaroos.

THREEFOLD MATERNITY

Kangaroos have a highly efficient pattern of reproduction. The young is born after a short gestation of one month. The newborn red kangaroo—one of the largest species—for example, is no more than 0.8 inches (2 centimeters) long. Unable to see, it crawls into its mother's pouch. Once

The slow and winsome koala spends its life clinging to the trunks of eucalyptus trees. The single young remains in the pouch for four or five months, and is then carried on its mother's back until it becomes independent.

Koala

inside, it clamps its mouth to a small teat to which it remains firmly attached until it is well developed, which takes about 7 months. Then it leaves the pouch, but keeps suckling milk from a second, larger teat. In the meantime the female has given birth to another baby kangaroo, housed in the pouch, and while all this is going on, a fertilized egg is already waiting in the oviduct, its development arrested until the pouch is left empty by the previous occupant.

WALKING ON FIVE LEGS: THE TAIL

Another typical feature of the kangaroo is its long, cylindrical and heavy tail, used mainly for locomotion. When the animal is moving slowly the tail is utilized as a fifth leg, helping to support its body weight, but when leaping the tail is extended behind to balance the upper part of the body, rather like the dinosaurs did many millions of years ago.

Among the Australian marsupials there are many examples of parallelism, or convergence, with the placental forms of the northern hemisphere, bearing witness to the marvelous flexibility of evolution. Marsupial mice and rats, flying squirrels, wolves, moles, dormice, cats and anteaters can all be found with equivalents among the rodents, carnivores and edentates that occupy the same ecological niches. Right: three significant examples.

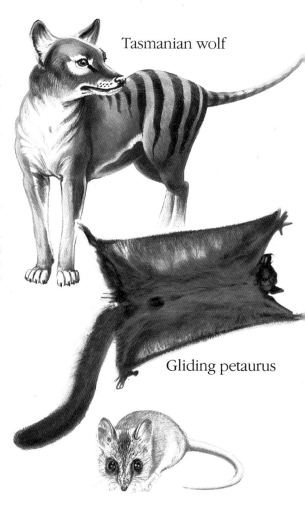

Tasmanian wolf

Gliding petaurus

Musky rat kangaroo

26

Sequence showing how a joey enters its mother's pouch, turning a sort of somersault.

1

2

3

4

Grey kangaroo

Below: in order to browse in open country — where they are exposed to attack from predators — kangaroos, like all herbivores, have evolved a fast run, although an unusual one: hopping. Leaning their body forward, they rise off their feet onto the tips of their toes. Both feet move forward together. They no longer use their arms, but hold them close to their chest. The heavy tail extended behind balances the upper parts of the body. In this way the kangaroos are able to attain a speed of nearly 40 miles (60 kilometers) per hour.

In the oval: the joey sticks its head out of the pouch for the first time some 5 months after entering it.

Below: in periods of drought, when food is scarce, it is normal for a female kangaroo to have dependent young at three different stages of development at the same time: a joey that has already left the pouch but which is still suckling, a newly born one that is permanently attached to the teat in her pouch, and a fertilized egg in the oviduct which is waiting for the pouch to be vacated by its previous occupant in order to begin development.

Red kangaroo

Left: a fight between two male red kangaroos. Kangaroos are very peaceful animals that rarely fight and then only over a female. In this case the two animals circle one another, making a series of moves and blows just like boxers, until one of them, leaning back on its tail, kicks out powerfully at its opponent with its hind legs.

27

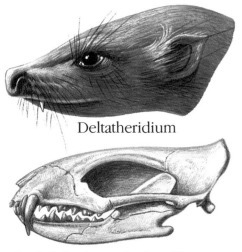

Deltatheridium

Fossil skull and reconstruction of the
Deltatheridium, an ancient placental
mammal that lived in the Cretaceous
Period at the same time as the dinosaurs.

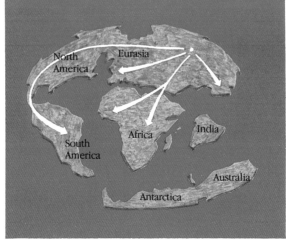

Center of origin — corresponding roughly to
present-day Mongolia — and migrations of
the placental mammals.

14. THE GREAT EXTINCT PLACENTAL MAMMALS

Summarizing the information available to us on the development of the placental mammals, and which we have touched on in previous chapters, let us recall that the placentals evolved from the pantotherians (see Chapter 9) over 100 million years ago. For a certain period they remained small animals similar to modern insectivores, confined to the nocturnal habitat owing to the overwhelming dominance of the dinosaurs. When the latter became extinct, about 65 million years ago, they began their expansion and evolution. Over a period of a few million years, small insectivores living in the north of the Eurasian continent, perhaps in the region of present-day Mongolia, gave rise not only to all the modern orders, but also to many others, now extinct. The speed of mammalian evolution over that period has something of the incredible about it, and yet the fact remains: the main lines of evolution among the placental mammals that dominate the earth today were settled in a very short time.

ANOTHER BIBLICAL MIGRATION

From Eurasia the placentals commenced their conquest of the entire planet, migrating to the various continents and easily supplanting the forms that already inhabited them, like the great flightless birds and the marsupials. They spread into Africa and, crossing the Bering Strait, first into North and then South America. However they were unable to reach Antarctica and Australia, since they were already isolated from the rest of the lands above sea level. As South and North America were subsequently split apart, evolution of the placental mammals in the two landmasses proceeded independently over a long span of time.

GIGANTISM

As had happened with other classes (amphibians, reptiles and birds) gigantic forms appeared among the placental mammals too. Plenty of food, lack of competition and predators always leads, with the passing of generations, to a progressive increase in size.

Indricotherium

The *Indricotherium* lived in Asia during the Oligocene
Period. It was a gigantic creature that browsed on the
leaves of the few trees to be found on the vast grassy
steppes. It belonged to an extinct branch of the
evolutionary line of the rhinoceroses. Its fossil remains
have been found in Kazakhstan
and on the shores of the Aral Sea.

28

Toxodon

Fossil skeleton of the *Toxodon*, a 9-foot (3-meter) long notoungulate that lived in Argentina during the Pliocene Period. The notoungulates are primitive representatives of the modern ungulates.

THE *INDRICOTHERIUM*

Resembling a rather ungainly giraffe, this extinct placental mammal actually belonged to the evolutionary line of rhinoceroses, and lived in the Kazakhstan region of Asia. It was a huge animal, perhaps the largest placental mammal ever to appear on land. Its head rose to 20 feet (6 meters) in height, while its length exceeded 52 feet (16 meters); the modern rhinoceros would have been able to pass beneath its belly without grazing it with its horn! Only the *Baluchitherium*, which belonged to the same evolutionary branch, could have competed with it for size. The success of these giants was short-lived; by about 30 million years ago they had already disappeared.

THE *ARSINOITHERIUM*

In appearance it was similar to the rhinoceros, despite being quite unrelated to it. Its classification is uncertain, considered akin to the proboscideans by some, but placed in a separate order by others. This powerful animal, over 10 feet (3 meters) in length, lived in North Africa during the Eocene Period, some 45-50 million years ago. If one considers that it appeared only 15 million years after the primitive insectivores, one gets an idea of the inexplicable speed of evolution over that period. Just as it had mysteriously and suddenly appeared, this placental became extinct, without leaving descendants.

THE *BRONTOTHERIUM*

Equally ancient was the *Brontotherium* with its peculiar Y-shaped horn, which lived in North America. Numerous fossil remains have revealed that it lived in herds. The *Brontotherium* shows clear affinities with the perissodactyls and is therefore connected to the evolutionary line that was to lead to the horse.

THE NOTOUNGULATES

These belonged to a sterile evolutionary branch which became extinct without leaving any progeny. The *Toxodon* was a representative of this order that lived in South America, during the Tertiary Era; it became extinct less than 10 million years ago.

THE *MEGATHERIUM*

The isolation of South America allowed some primitive placental mammals to expand freely and to attain bizarre forms and dimensions. The *Megatherium* is one example. It belonged to an order of mammals, the edentates, which have always found life difficult in other parts of the world and yet managed to reach a considerable size in the South American environment: 23 feet (7 meters) in length and a height similar to that of the elephant. It must have moved sluggishly, just enough to get from one shrub to another, as its basic food was leaves. Its small brain suggests that its intelligence was limited, and yet this edentate not only thrived in its land of origin but also spread to North America when the two continents were reunited.

Arsinoitherium

The *Arsinoitherium* bore two massive horns on its forehead and led an amphibious life. Fossils of this strange animal which lived towards the end of the Eocene Period (see also Ch. 19), have been found only in Egypt.

29

European water shrew

Hedgehog

Mole

Potamogale

The illustration above shows a selection of European insectivores. The mole digs long underground tunnels, in which it locates the nest for its young and hoards its food supplies. The hedgehog lives above ground, in dry and bushy terrain. The water shrew lives on the banks of ditches and streams.

The potamogale is an insectivore found along rivers throughout equatorial Africa. It is nocturnal and spends much of its life in the water.

15. INSECTIVORES, EDENTATES AND PHOLIDOTA

THE INSECTIVORES

This is the most primitive order of placental mammals. The modern insectivores' skull and teeth, size and habits are very similar to those of the ancient, small, nocturnal insectivores that lived along with dinosaurs. Evidence for their primitive nature is also provided by the small brain with a perfectly smooth surface and a very low volume. Conversely their senses of touch, smell and hearing are very efficient. The insectivores, which are all predators, are in turn actively hunted by nocturnal birds of prey and by many carnivores.

If one were to choose the most aggressive, courageous and ferocious predator in the animal kingdom, the tiny European water shrew would certainly come high on the list. Its high rate of metabolism and energy requirements—every day it has to eat a quantity of meat equal to double its weight—oblige it to hunt continuously throughout the night and even to attack animals two or three times its size.

Among the insectivores, the *Erinaceidae* and *Tenrecidae* families have a coat of long, stiff hairs, modified into horny spines. The European hedgehog, for example, when frightened rolls into a ball, so that the spines, which are present only on its back, protect its head, legs and the soft underparts. The hedgehogs attack, kill and eat even such poisonous animals as bees, wasps, hornets and vipers.

The *Talpidae* family, which includes the European and American moles, is specialized in hunting underground. The mole digs a system of long burrows in grasslands, searching for earthworms, only guided by its powerful sense of smell and touch.

The potamogale on the other hand belongs to a family that has specialized in hunting in the water of streams and ponds. Its shape is similar to that of an

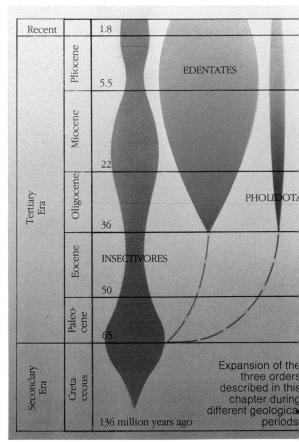

Recent		1.8
Tertiary Era	Pliocene	5.5 EDENTATES
	Miocene	22
	Oligocene	36 PHOLIDOTA
	Eocene	50 INSECTIVORES
	Paleo-cene	65
Secondary Era	Creta-ceous	136 million years ago

Expansion of the three orders described in this chapter during different geological periods

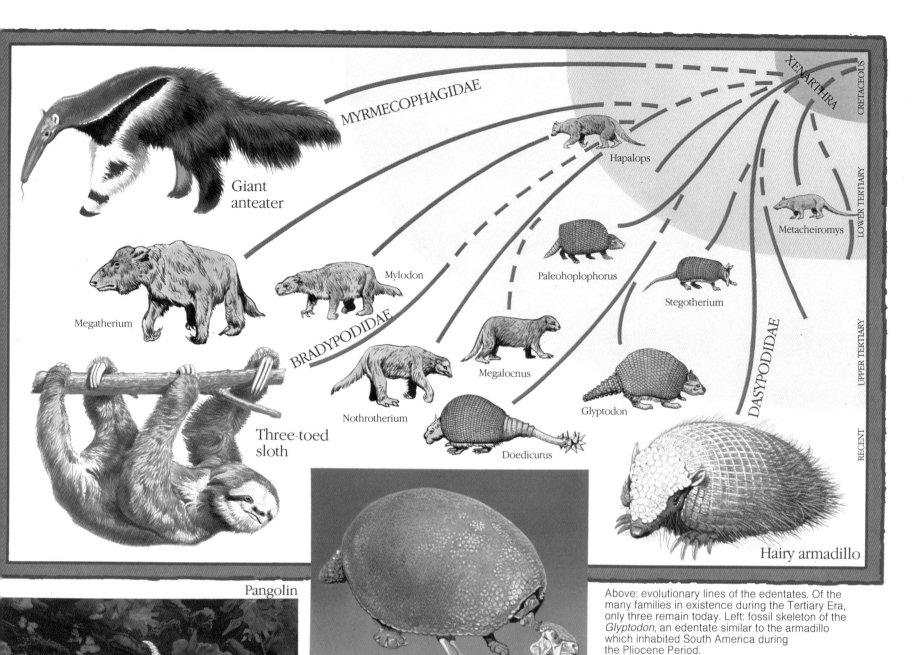

Giant anteater

MYRMECOPHAGIDAE

Hapalops

XENARTHRA

CRETACEOUS

Metacheiromys

LOWER TERTIARY

Megatherium

Mylodon

Paleohoplophorus

Stegotherium

BRADYPODIDAE

UPPER TERTIARY

Megalocnus

Glyptodon

DASYPODIDAE

Three-toed sloth

Nothrotherium

Doedicurus

RECENT

Hairy armadillo

Pangolin

Above: evolutionary lines of the edentates. Of the many families in existence during the Tertiary Era, only three remain today. Left: fossil skeleton of the *Glyptodon*, an edentate similar to the armadillo which inhabited South America during the Pliocene Period.

otter and ideally suited for swimming, assisted by the movements of the long, laterally compressed tail.

THE EDENTATES

The order of edentates (from the Latin word meaning "without teeth") was highly successful in South America, even with gigantic forms, such as the *Megatherium* (see Chapter 14). The armadillos, anteaters and sloths are the only survivors of the order, all of which live in the area of their origin, South and Central America.

The armadillo belongs to an evolutionary line that has developed a system of defense based on a heavy armor, made of bony plates, that covers the whole body, including head and tail. This group too has produced gigantic forms, such as the *Glyptodon*, almost 13 feet (4 meters) long. A close, and no less gigantic relative, the *Doedicurus*, also had a powerful tail with a club bristling with spines at the end. In spite

of their means of defense, these two edentates became extinct 10-15 million years ago.

The anteater of swamps and savannas in Central and South America is the only edentate that really has no teeth in its elongated snout; it tears open ant and termite nests with its powerful foreclaws and collects the exposed insects with its long and sticky tongue.

In the depths of the South American forests live the sloths, very peculiar animals that feed on leaves gathered from the branches with extremely slow movements. In fact they have no idea of haste; even when threatened, usually by large snakes, they are unable to move at speed and are therefore easily caught.

THE PANGOLINS

The bodies of these animals are covered with large, sharp-edged scales. The only representative of the *Pholidota* order, the pangolin lives in tropical Africa and Asia, feeding on ants and termites which it catches with its tiny, long and sticky tongue just like the American anteater. When attacked, it locks itself into a ball, so that the soft parts of the body are covered by the hard scales.

The order of the *Pholidota* contains only the family of the pangolins. These are nocturnal animals and some arboreal species are able to move through the branches with agility, hanging from their long tails.

31

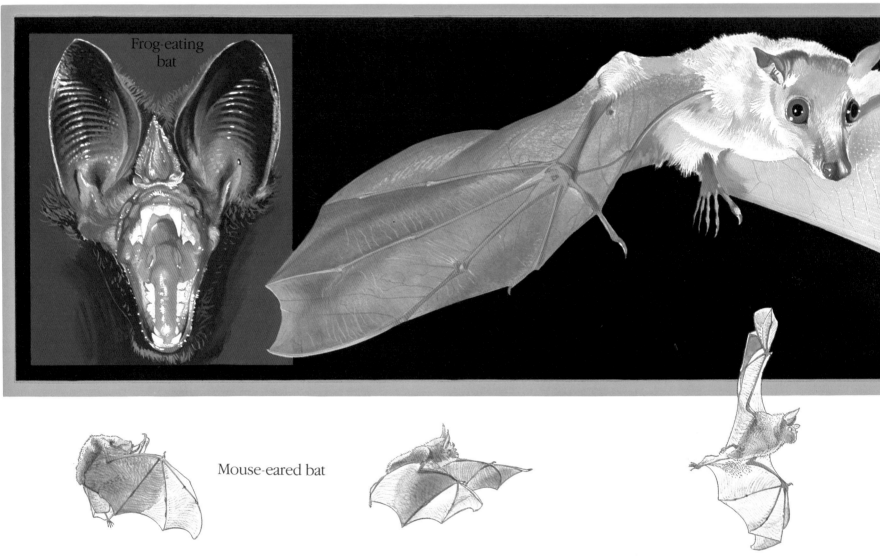

Frog-eating bat

Mouse-eared bat

16. CHIROPTERS

Though advancing triumphantly over the earth and into the water, in the air, placental mammals encountered an insuperable barrier. By the time they emerged, birds were highly developed, having attained a high degree of specialization for flight. For this reason the eutherian mammals could not supplant the birds in the skies as well. However most birds have diurnal habits, only a few of them, the nocturnal birds of prey, can live and hunt in the dark. This ecological niche was therefore still available to the mammals, especially those that lived on insects, ignored by the various members of the owl family.

THE ORIGIN

Hence from placental mammals a new order evolved capable of powered flight and of catching nocturnal insects on the wing: the chiropters. Their origin is uncertain, but they may well have derived from primitive insectivores. The fragility of the bat skeleton makes fossilization extremely unlikely, except for the skull and teeth, which are very similar to those of the insectivores. The first unquestionable fossil remains of chiropters date back to the Eocene Period, 40-45 million years ago. But the skeletal features of these finds are very similar to those of modern bats, which leads one to presume a much older origin.

THE TECHNIQUE OF FLIGHT

The flight of bats has some similarities to that of birds, and is perhaps closest to that of the hummingbirds, as some are able to hover motionless in the air. Their flight is always accomplished by flapping the wings: no bat is capable of gliding. Their seemingly fragile wings—composed of only two layers of delicate skin stretched between the limbs and powered by muscles in the chest—do not merely move up and down, but rotate and are pushed forward when lowered, almost meeting in front of the head, and backwards when raised. The frequency of the wingbeat is not very high, 15-20 beats a minute, and the average speed does not exceed 12 miles (20 kilometers) per hour.

Inset, top left: the chiropters have long and sharp canines and large highly sensitive ears.

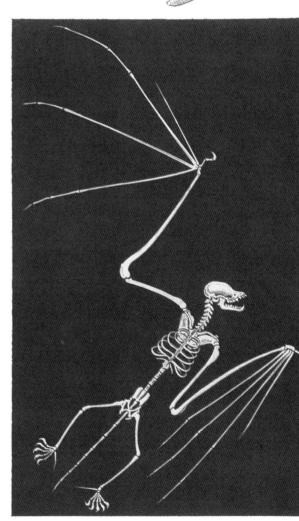

Right: the slender skeleton of a bat shows how the wing is supported by four greatly elongated digits of the forelimb. Top center: the wings, or patagia, are made of a very thin membrane of tough and elastic skin, rich in nerve endings and blood vessels.

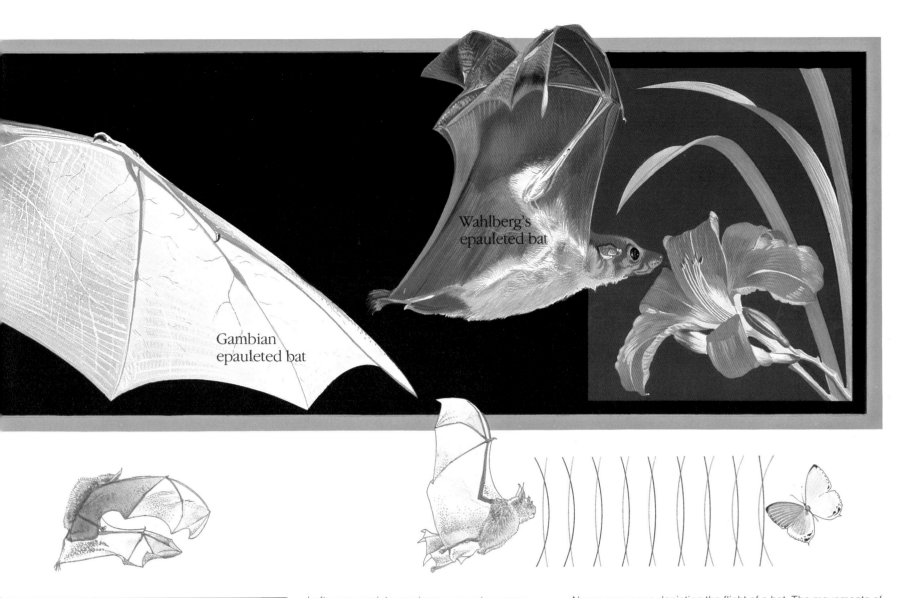

Wahlberg's epauleted bat

Gambian epauleted bat

Left: some mainly carnivorous species swoop down on their prey from above. Others (inset, top right) feed on the nectar of flowers, performing a crucial task of pollination.

Above: sequence depicting the flight of a bat. The movements of the wing follow an elliptical path. The animal, which is usually nocturnal, detects the presence of an obstacle, or of its prey, by picking up echoes from the ultrasounds that it emits.

False vampire

The chiropters have a powerful social instinct. While resting during the day, or in hibernation, they hang upside down in large groups from the branches of trees or the roofs of caves.

THE NATURAL SONAR

Many bats orient themselves in flight by a technique that scientists call echolocation. They detect obstacles or prey in the dusky and dark surroundings by emitting ultrasonic sounds and assessing the sound waves bounced off. This natural sonar acts in different ways. In the vespertilionids the ultrasonic sounds are produced by the larynx and emitted from the open mouth. The more sophisticated rhinolophids emit sound waves from a peculiar horseshoe-shaped nose capable of movement, allowing the beam of waves to be sent in different directions; thus the mouth can be used to catch prey at the same time as sound waves are emitted. In order to pick up echoed-back sound waves accurately, bats have highly developed and sensitive ears, with two large and movable auricles, able to capture sound waves from any direction and collect them to the tympanic membrane.

FEEDING

The chiropters usually live on nocturnal insects caught on the wing, but there are plenty of exceptions, including some feeding habits truly unusual for a mammal. The glossophagines, or flower bats, for example, feed on nectar and pollen that they collect with their tongues while hovering in front of flowers. As they fly from flower to flower, these bats pollinate the plants, just like bees or butterflies. In the tropical regions of America live the desmodonts, better known as vampire bats, which suck the blood of other mammals without waking their sleeping victims up. Some bats, such as the bulldog bat, are skilled fishers in both fresh and saltwater; others, such as the false vampire, hunt small rodents.

RESTING

When not on the wing, bats take their rest in a really unusual position, hanging upside down from rocks or branches by their hind limbs. In this position, which would be uncomfortable for us, they pass the whole of the winter in hibernation; in order to reduce heat loss during this period, bats roost close together in caves.

33

Some of the many species of rodent are illustrated inside the blue frame. The black rat and the brown rat are distributed throughout the world. Rats are very intelligent and can be trained to carry out skill exercises. Porcupines, found in Italy, Asia and Africa, have a coat of bristles that turns along the back into a crest of long and stiff quills marked with light and dark rings. Beavers live in Europe and North America; herbivores, they can fell a birch with a diameter of 3 inches (8 centimeters) in five minutes; they build dams out of branches, mud and leaves to control the level of the pools in which they live. The squirrel is an arboreal animal that uses its long tail as a counterweight when leaping.

Expansion of the two orders in relation to geological periods.

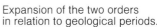

17. RODENTS AND LAGOMORPHS

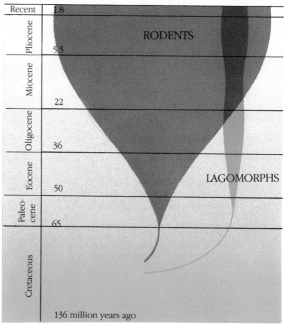

RODENTS

This is the largest order of placental mammals, comprising over half the total number of mammalian species. Some of the best known are squirrels, beavers, marmots, hamsters, dormice, porcupines, guinea-pigs, gophers, etc. Some species (the rat springs to mind) can be found almost everywhere in the world, in numbers that run into the billions. They are generally small in size, but range from the 2 inch (5 centimeter) long harvest mouse, which climbs ears of wheat to gather the seeds, to the 35 inches (90 centimeters) of the South American capybara. The great success of the rodents is due to the absence of any kind of specialization, accompanied by their readiness to adapt to any kind of environment and food; they also have a high degree of intelligence, which permits them to constantly modify their strategies for survival.

FEEDING AND HABITS

The name rodents comes from the Latin *rodere*, to gnaw, and from these animals' habit of gnawing at anything. Their incisor teeth are long, chisel-shaped and never stop growing, so the animal is obliged to gnaw in order to wear them down; the molars on the other hand are flat and adapted for grinding the food finely. They have a long intestine for digestion. Food of vegetable origin is generally preferred, but they do not reject meat or, in case of necessity, anything that they can digest.

Most rodents are nocturnal animals, thus their most developed senses are hearing, smell and touch, especially with the long vibrissae located on the head. Usually they have no means of defense. For survival they rely on caution and their innate timidity, which causes them to flee at the slightest hint of danger. Nonetheless rodents form the prey of reptiles, birds

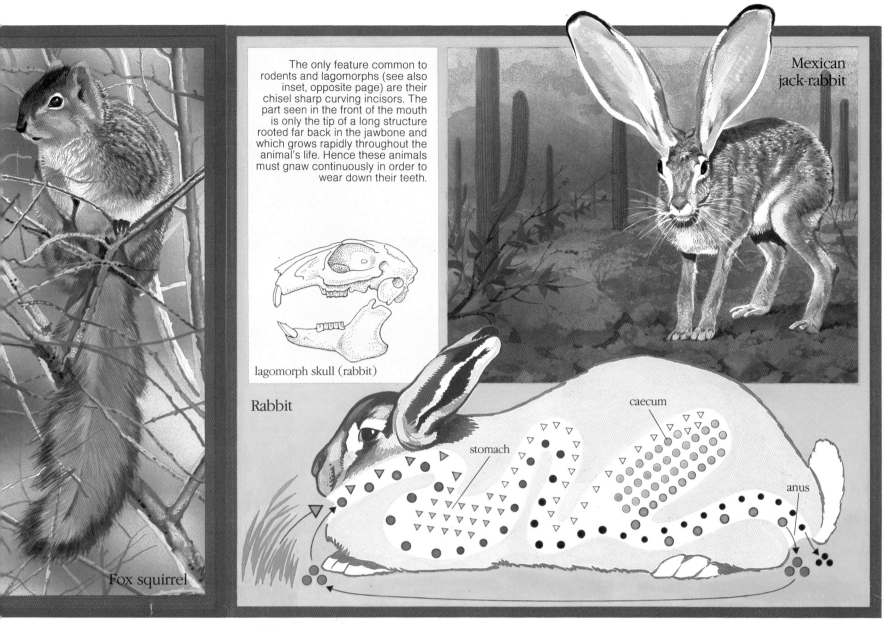

The only feature common to rodents and lagomorphs (see also inset, opposite page) are their chisel sharp curving incisors. The part seen in the front of the mouth is only the tip of a long structure rooted far back in the jawbone and which grows rapidly throughout the animal's life. Hence these animals must gnaw continuously in order to wear down their teeth.

lagomorph skull (rabbit)

Rabbit

Mexican jack-rabbit

Fox squirrel

caecum

stomach

anus

The hare and the rabbit are typical representatives of the lagomorphs, found on every continent. To get the most out of their food they use a strange method known as caecotrophism. The ingested plant matter is partially digested by the stomach and the caecum. In the latter it is formed into pellets, expelled from the anus and immediately swallowed again. In this way the plant matter passes through the animal's body twice, yielding up all its nutritive substances.

and mammals that either hunt at night or seek them out in their hiding-places. Rodents make up for this continual slaughter with a high birth-rate and very rapid embryonal development. A pair of mice may produce a dozen offspring at a time, at intervals of about 40 days. The young begin breeding a few weeks after birth. If they were not held in check by predators, the rodents would have taken over a long time ago.

The usefulness of rodents is limited. Some species (such as the chinchilla and the beaver) have valuable fur coats. Other rodents cause damage on a scale that can reach worrisome proportions. Rats, for instance, devour enormous quantities of cereals and are disease carriers.

WARS AMONG RATS

To describe all the rodents would be an encyclopedic task. Here we will tell the story of the rat, owing to its close relationship with man. When prehistoric nomadic hunters began to settle in permanent homes in order to practice agriculture, the black rat (*Rattus*

rattus) decided that living at the expense of man's labor was far simpler and safer than living wild. So it installed itself in every human habitation, even taking passage on ships and thereby spreading round the globe. During the Middle Ages life became difficult for the black rat when the brown rat (*Rattus norvegicus*) arrived from China-Mongolia. A clash between the two species was inevitable and the victorious brown rat succeeded in driving the black rat out of human houses and taking its place. The brown rat prefers sewers, cellars and damp places, while the black rat has been relegated to dry places such as attics. The struggle between man and rat (whether brown or black) is of very ancient origin. The strategies adopted by each side are constantly evolving and improving, but victory will never smile on either.

THE LAGOMORPHS

Their similarity to rodents is confined to their long and continuously growing incisors. The lagomorphs have no philogenetic relationship with the rodents;

they may in fact belong to the evolutionary line of the ungulates, or to an autonomous collateral line. The hare and rabbit, which are the most common species, originally inhabited only Europe, Africa and North America, but man has introduced them into the other continents as well, because of their importance in hunting and the quality of their meat. In Australia rabbits, in the absence of natural predators, have reproduced so fast that they have turned into a genuine scourge.

The lagomorphs prefer a vegetarian diet, which they can digest perfectly thanks to a peculiarity of their intestines and their feeding habits: caecotrophism. The food, ground up by the teeth, passes into the intestine where the difficult process of digesting plant matter commences and comes to a halt in a long caecal appendix. Here the contents are converted into spherules that are excreted during the night and immediately swallowed again by the animal, so that the food makes a second passage through the intestine. By this means the plant matter is broken down completely and its nutritional properties are utilized to the maximum.

18.
PERISSODACTYLS AND ARTIODACTYLS
(Ungulates)

The ungulates superorder comprises those placental mammals that touch the ground with the ends of their phalanges. This evolutionary trend emerged to increase speed (see Chapter 8). In fact there are many ungulate species capable of running at speed over long distances. However this mode of locomotion means that the whole weight of the body is carried by the nail, which has become greatly enlarged in ungulates, turning into a hoof.

ORIGIN

The ungulates emerged a long time ago; a few million years after the extinction of the dinosaurs, at the beginning of the Tertiary Era, an evolutionary branch of herbivores, the *Condylarthra*, appeared with the fundamental features of the superorder. After this, however, many other branches emerged. Only two orders of ungulates have survived: the perissodactyls and the artiodactyls. The perissodactyls touch the ground with an *odd* number of toes, the artiodactyls with an *even* number.

PERISSODACTYLS

The most typical representative of this order is the horse, belonging to the *Equidae* family, mentioned in every text dealing with evolution (see *The Evolution of Life* volume in this series, Chapters 9 and 26). In fact the horse is well suited to illustrate the flexibility of the organization of living creatures. It is one of the few animals that man has succeeded in domesticating. Through crossbreeding, over the span of a few centuries, man produced almost opposite races; in some strength and power has been augmented, in others speed and agility. A very close relative of the horse is the ass and the two can even interbreed, but the offspring, called a mule if the mother is a horse, or a hinny if the mother is an ass, is sterile.

The African *Equidae*, the zebras, touch the ground only with the nail of the third toe, transformed into a powerful hoof. The other two perissodactyl families, the *Rhinocerontidae* and the *Tapiridae*, still have five differently developed toes. The rhinoceroses are the only living perissodactyls with a horn made up of small horny cylinders cemented together.

Four species of tapirs exist: three are to be found in the tropical forests of South America; the fourth, the Malay tapir, inhabits lowlands in southern Asia, especially swampy forests. This species was only classified in the 19th century by the French naturalist Georges Cuvier. Tapirs place the third toe of the foot on the ground. The onager, also known as the Central Asian wild ass, lives in the steppes and desert plateaus of northern Iran. It has a long and thick coat in winter and a smooth and glossy one in the summer. Only a few hundred of these animals survive in the wild state.

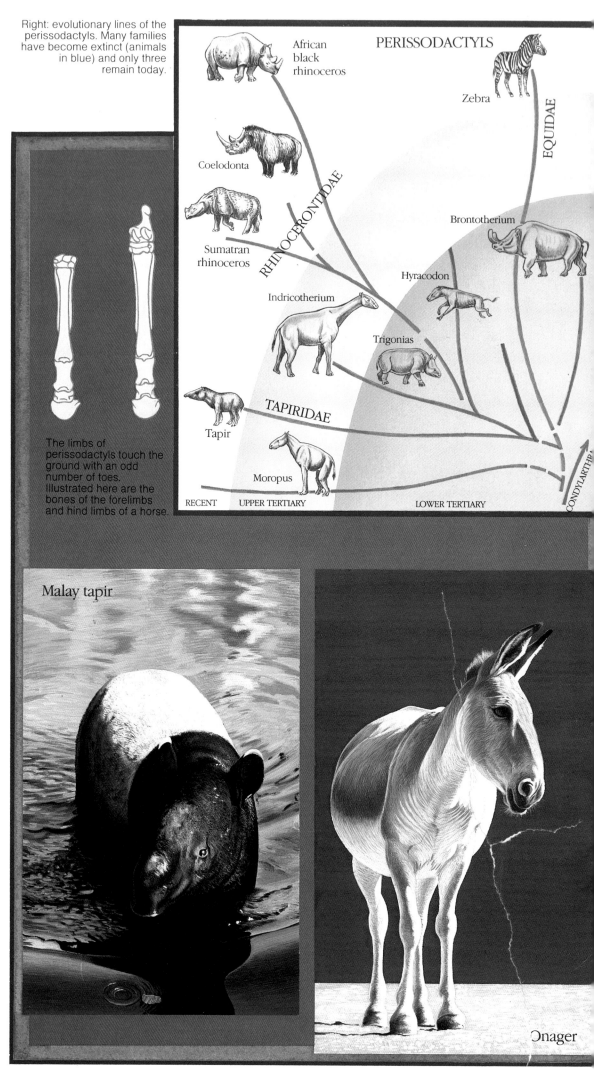

Right: evolutionary lines of the perissodactyls. Many families have become extinct (animals in blue) and only three remain today.

The limbs of perissodactyls touch the ground with an odd number of toes. Illustrated here are the bones of the forelimbs and hind limbs of a horse.

Malay tapir

Onager

36

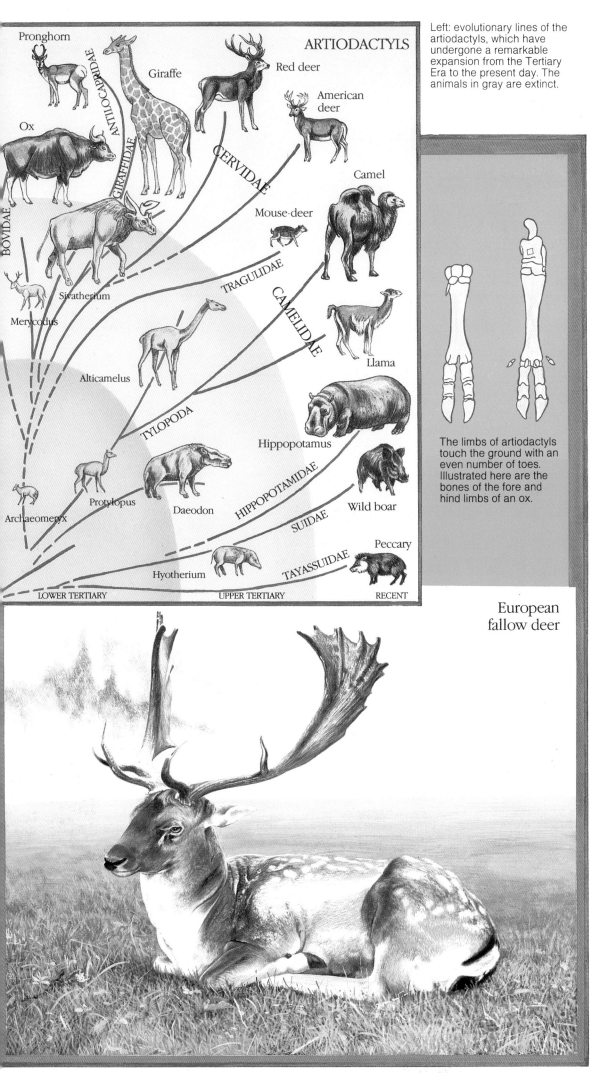

ARTIODACTYLS

Pronghorn · Giraffe · Red deer · American deer · Ox · ANTILOCAPRIDAE · GIRAFFIDAE · BOVIDAE · CERVIDAE · Camel · Mouse-deer · Sivatherium · Merycodus · TRAGULIDAE · CAMELIDAE · Altikamelus · Llama · TYLOPODA · Hippopotamus · HIPPOPOTAMIDAE · Protylopus · Daeodon · Wild boar · SUIDAE · Archaeomeryx · Peccary · Hyotherium · TAYASSUIDAE

LOWER TERTIARY · UPPER TERTIARY · RECENT

Left: evolutionary lines of the artiodactyls, which have undergone a remarkable expansion from the Tertiary Era to the present day. The animals in gray are extinct.

The limbs of artiodactyls touch the ground with an even number of toes. Illustrated here are the bones of the fore and hind limbs of an ox.

European fallow deer

The fallow deer closely resembles the red deer, but has antlers in the shape of a broad and flattened blade, while those of the red deer are circular in cross-section throughout their length. All the *Cervidae* shed their antlers every year, regrowing them the next year but to a greater length and with more branches. During growth the antlers are supplied with blood through vessels in a covering of skin, known as "velvet," which is then rubbed off on trees or the ground. The summer coat of the fallow deer is covered with white spots. It inhabits open woods in Europe, where it feeds on the leaves of trees and bushes and acorns.

THE RUMINANT ARTIODACTYLS

The expansion and evolutionary success of this order (comprising the *Bovidae, Cervidae, Giraffidae, Antilocapridae* and *Tragulidae* families) is perhaps due to the stomach, specialized for efficient digestion of the cellulose in plant matter (see Chapter 7).

The main problem faced by a herbivore is not that of obtaining food, which is generally within easy reach, but of avoiding becoming food for a predator. To defend themselves the ruminants have evolved different strategies: buffaloes and oxen have a sturdy build and powerful horns, antelopes and gazelles are nimble and fleet runners, mouse-deer, no larger than a rabbit, remain concealed in the undergrowth.

The ruminants display a wide variety of horns. Even the great giraffe has two small bony horns covered with skin, apparently useless, but which may be a hangover from the animal's forebears. Usually the male *Cervidae* (deer, moose, elks, caribous, roe-bucks...) have large branching horns known as antlers. These are entirely bony and are cast each autumn, to regrow larger each spring. The *Bovidae* (oxen, buffalo, bison, wildebeest, yaks, goats, sheep, steinbocks, antelopes, oryxes, gazelles...), sometimes both sexes, sometimes only males, have twin horns made of a bony shaft covered by a horny case; these horns do not drop off periodically but grow in step with the animal.

THE NON-RUMINANT ARTIODACTYLS

These include the *Suidae, Tayassuidae* (peccary) and *Hippopotamidae* families, which are apparently very different from one another. The economic importance of pigs as a food source for man is easily grasped; these animals were among the first to be domesticated by prehistoric man, who preferred to raise them at home instead of hunting dangerous wild boars amidst the perils of the forest. The hippopotamus, on the other hand, still inhabits the African wild, especially the equatorial belt, wherever there is sufficient water, for it leads a totally amphibian life.

TYLOPOD ARTIODACTYLS

This suborder includes the *Camelidae* family, represented by the llamas in South America, and the camels and the dromedaries in North Africa and Asia. Camels and dromedaries are highly resistant to harsh climates, whether hot, cold or extremely dry. As a result they have become invaluable partners for men inhabiting difficult territories.

37

From the ancient order of the *Condylarthra*, which lived during the Paleocene Period and were the progenitors of all the ungulates, derive the collateral branches of three orders extinct today, the amblypods with the *Uintatherium*, the pantodonts with the *Coryphodon* and the embrithopods with the *Arsinoitherium*, as well as the superorder of the subungulates with three orders that are still in existence today: the hyracoids, sirenians and proboscideans. In the evolutionary line of the latter we find mammals with a proboscis that lived in different eras and are now extinct, such as the *Moeritherium*, *Gomphotherium*, *Dinotherium*, Mammoth and *Mastodon*.

Hyrax

19. PROBOSCIDEANS, HYRACOIDS, SIRENIANS

HYRACOIDS

Mastodon

THE PROBOSCIDEANS

An important evolutionary path taken by the mammals, that of the subungulates, includes the modern elephants. It is possible to reconstruct the main stages in the evolution of these animals beginning with the *Condylarthra*, the probable progenitors of all the ungulates. The changes that have occurred along this path are various: the skull has grown considerably shorter, while the bulk of the animal has increased progressively; the incisors have also grown, to the point of forming long and powerful tusks. In some cases, such as the elephants, only the upper incisors have lengthened, in others, such as the *Dinotherium*, only the lower ones, while in yet others both grew longer, as in the *Paleomastodon*. The proboscis, or trunk, derives from a fusion of the nose with the upper lip and is utilized not only for smelling but also as a prehensile organ.

Among the largest living terrestrial mammals, the elephants are split into two different species, the Indian and the African elephant.

Tusks are missing in the Indian female and fairly small in the male. Their ears are small and triangular. Indian elephants are generally docile, easy to domesticate and to exploit for heavy work.

The African elephant, found today in Africa, is distinguishable by its large and constantly moving ears, which cool the blood that circulates through them.

All elephants are strictly herbivorous and adapt themselves to eating anything, even the bark of trees, which they detach with the aid of their tusks and trunk. The food is carefully masticated by a single large tooth which grows in the shape of a large dental plate on each half of the lower and upper jaw. This tooth is periodically replaced by a new one as the old is worn away, but not past the animal's 60th year. If it manages to survive its natural enemies, which are parasites rather than predators, and the elephant loses its last tooth, no longer capable of mastication, it literally dies of hunger.

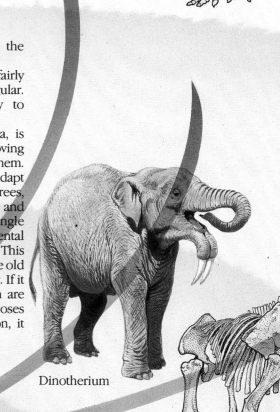
Dinotherium

Gomphotherium

Moeritherium

Subungulates
from the
CONDYLARTHRA

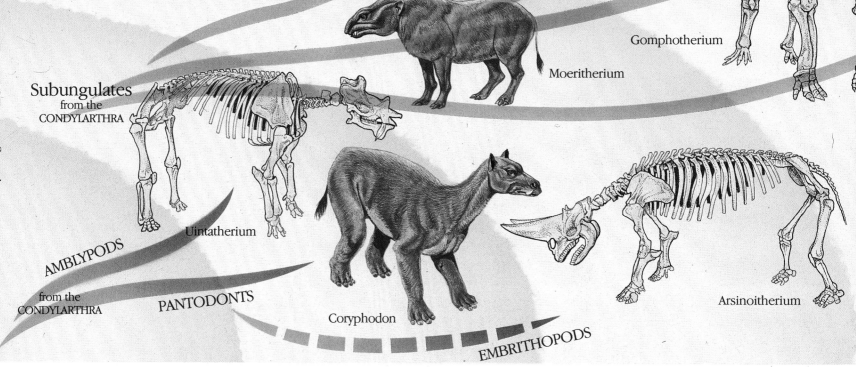

AMBLYPODS

Uintatherium

from the
CONDYLARTHRA

PANTODONTS

Coryphodon

Arsinoitherium

EMBRITHOPODS

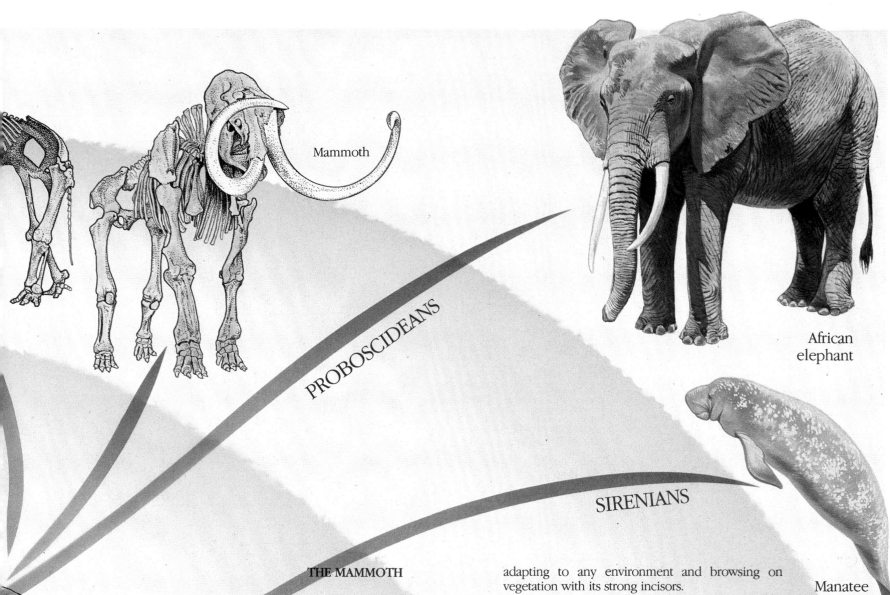

Mammoth

PROBOSCIDEANS

African
elephant

SIRENIANS

Manatee
or sea cow

THE MAMMOTH

In the Pleistocene Period, the earth was inhabited by a third species of proboscidean, the mammoth, which was frequently the prey of our hunting ancestors. Living in Siberia and Alaska, it had an abundant coat of fur to protect it from the cold and two exceptionally long and curved tusks. Its extinction was probably caused by the most recent glaciation; the cold became unbearable even for these enormous animals and, being unable to migrate to a more favorable climate (although the reason for this is unclear), they were doomed to die out.

THE HYRACOIDS

The evolutionary line of the subungulates also includes the small order of hyracoids, or hyraxes. The form and living habits of these small mammals are similar to those of the rodents, although they are closely related to elephants. The hyrax lives in Africa,

adapting to any environment and browsing on vegetation with its strong incisors.

THE SIRENIANS

Together with pinnipeds (Chapter 21) and cetaceans (Chapter 22), though with less success, sirenians, or sea cows, were the only placental mammals who colonized the aquatic environment. They live in coastal waters or large rivers and feed upon marine or freshwater plants, as their diet is totally herbivorous. Swimming is accomplished by the highly developed and powerful tail, while the hind limbs have vanished and the forelimbs have been transformed into broad flippers.

Today the sea cows are represented by the manatee living in the Americas and Africa, and by the dugong, found in Africa, India and Australia. Another species of the Bering Sea, the Steller's sea cow, over 23 feet (7 meters) in length, was exterminated by man when whaling started in the 18th century.

The ancestors of the elephants have been the subject of much study, given the abundance of fossil remains. Thus we see a progressive regression of the nasal bones and changes in dentition and in the proportions of the skull. A new organ also appeared, the proboscis, which is used for respiration, perception of odors, the gathering of food and water, as a highly sensitive tactile organ and as an arm of defense and offense.

Phenacodus	Moeritherium	Paleomastodon	Stegomastodon	Elephas
Primitive condylarthran	Eocene	Oligocene	Pliocene-Pleistocene	Today

Smilodon

Zebra

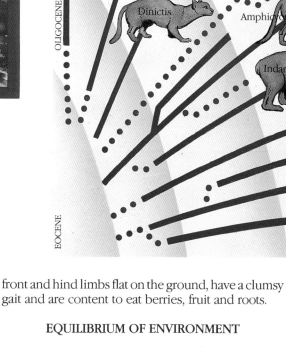

Hyena

Civet

Mongoose

Smilodon

Ictitherium

Dinictis

Amphicyon

Indarcto

HOLOCENE

PLEISTOCENE

PLIOCENE

MIOCENE

OLIGOCENE

EOCENE

HYAENIDAE and PROTELIDAE

VIVERRIDAE

HERPESTIDAE

One of the great extinct carnivores was the *Smilodon*, which lived in North America and Argentina during the Pleistocene Period, with curved canine teeth that were nearly 6 inches (14 centimeters) long. The inset depicts a fossil skull of this animal found at Rancho la Brea (Los Angeles). This was the site of a bituminous lake on whose surface rainwater used to collect. Animals that came to drink became trapped in the tar which assisted the process of fossilization.

20. FISSIPED CARNIVORES

ORIGINS

The order of the carnivores is a very ancient one, which appeared on the earth as far back as the Paleocene Period, some 60 million years ago, as a further specialization of the primitive insectivores. The shape of the molars in these two orders is very similar, especially in the oldest forms. In the course of evolution, the teeth of the carnivores became sharper and more pointed in order to tear off and coarsely masticate strips of meat. At the same time the canines tended to grow longer so as to inflict deep wounds on the victim. In the gradually evolving forms, the upper canines became larger and longer; in some cases, such as the *Smilodon* and *Machairodus* (species of sabre-toothed tigers), they attained lengths of 12-16 inches (30-40 centimeters). This potent weapon could only be used with the mouth stretched wide open. It is interesting to note that the same kind of huge canine also developed among the marsupials (the *Thylacosmilus*).

GENERAL FEATURES

The modern carnivores are divided into two suborders: the fissipeds live on land, the pinnipeds have adapted themselves to marine environments (see Chapter 21). Both are distinguished by an exclusively or predominantly carnivorous diet. This means that their food has to be caught and torn to pieces: hence the development in the fissipeds of an agile body with a highly flexible spinal column and limbs adapted for running. They touch the ground only with their toes, provided with sharp claws. In some species these can be retracted when not in use, to prevent them from being worn down. Very high speeds may be attained; the cheetah, for example, the fastest of all mammals, is capable of bursts of up to 68 miles (110 kilometers) per hour. However this speed can only be maintained for a very few minutes, and if the first attack is unsuccessful when hunting, the animal has to slow down and rest. Only the bears diverge from this model. They place the paws of both

front and hind limbs flat on the ground, have a clumsy gait and are content to eat berries, fruit and roots.

EQUILIBRIUM OF ENVIRONMENT

Wherever prey is to be found there are also predators. In fact there is a relationship of equilibrium between the different species in each community, an equilibrium that is constantly being adjusted. If by some happy circumstance, the number of herbivores increases above the normal level, the greater availability of food brings within a few years (or months, depending on the type of animals involved) an increase in the number of carnivores. These in turn reduce the number of herbivores, and the shortage of prey slows down the rate of reproduction of the carnivores, allowing the herbivores to increase in number again, and so on. If one of the two groups

40

Tiger

Cat

Cheetah

Dog

Fox

Jackal

Bear

Panda

Raccoon

Badger

Marten

Otter

FELIDAE

CANIDAE

AILURIDAE

PROCYONIDAE

MUSTELIDAE

Evolutionary lines of the fissiped carnivores in relation to geological periods.

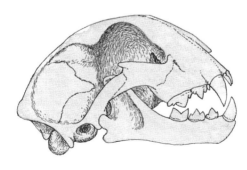

Skull of a modern cheetah, showing a considerable shortening of the vicious canines. In carnivores the lower jaw can only move up and down, and not from side to side as in man.

Bengal tiger

The beauty of the Bengal tiger reflected in the waters of an Indian tropical forest; the remains of a carcass can be seen on the bank. It is the tiger's habit to carry freshly-killed prey to a river or pool before consuming it, for they need to drink often when eating. Their hunger satisfied, they cover the remains with grass and leaves and then lie down to rest.

were ever to gain the upper hand, the population would destroy itself. The ecological pyramid or food chain is built up of a succession of bigger and bigger consumers until one reaches the large carnivores, which are not preyed on by any animal and die from parasites or old age, when they are no longer capable of feeding themselves.

HUNTING

The capture of prey requires particular skill, since the animal preyed on has also developed a series of defensive stratagems over the course of its evolution. In carnivores the brain is highly developed and its surface is heavily furrowed and convoluted, a sign of high intelligence as has already been pointed out. Play, as we saw in Chapter 6, is highly developed in young carnivores and is based largely on simulated hunts, attacks and ambushes. Such activity continues in the adult as well, as pure amusement. The otter for example is famous for its ability to play for hours, whether alone or in a group. By playing games, the young animal learns the basic techniques for procuring food, which will then be perfected in actual

experience. Carnivores are not bound by stereotyped patterns of behavior predetermined for each species but, thanks to their intelligence, can change their hunting strategies according to circumstances.

PACKS

Many carnivores (wolves, hyenas, lions) live in small packs, in which a precise hierarchical order is established between individual members. On the whole, pack life is advantageous, because the pack, following carefully studied techniques, may isolate, attack and kill prey that are bigger, stronger and faster than individual members. Wolves, for example, hunt the elk, African wild dogs pursue the wildebeest, and hyenas kill the zebra. Conversely, the species in which the animals are lone hunters, like the leopard, content themselves with prey no larger than they.

But life in packs also has its disadvantages. Among the lions, for example, a young male, when about three years old, is compelled by the ruling male to leave the pack. And if it is true that hunting as a group facilitates the capture of food, it is also true that the weakest individuals often only get poor and insufficient remnants of food.

41

21. PINNIPED CARNIVORES

This suborder of the carnivores appeared in the Miocene Period, about 25 million years ago. It probably derives from an offshoot of the ursids and/or the mustelids that was driven into the sea and specialized for aquatic life. It is composed of three families which share the finned feet: the *Phocidae* (true seals and elephant seals), the *Odobenidae* (walrues) and the *Otariidae* (sea lions).

SWIMMING

In the pinnipeds the hind limbs have been displaced backwards, the bones of the thigh and lower leg shortened and the feet broadened to the point of forming two large flippers. The forelimbs have also been transformed into flippers, which are used both for locomotion and for changing direction. Generally they have an ovoid, thickset and heavy body, from

heat loss is indispensable. In the penguins the plumage has been modified to form a continuous cover for the skin that insulates it from the water. This is not possible in the pinnipeds, as their fur is made up of short and stiff hairs that are totally inadequate as a protection from the cold. Insulation of the body is achieved instead by increasing the thickness of the layer of fatty tissue just below the surface of the skin. This layer, which can be several inches (centimeters) thick, insulates the muscles, internal organs, nervous system and blood from the external environment. A curious system is employed to keep the flippers and their related musculature warm, which have little fatty insulation. The artery that carries blood to flippers is surrounded by five veins through which the venous blood, warmed by muscular contractions in the flipper itself, returns to the body. In this way the arterial blood is also preserved from heat loss.

REPRODUCTION

However well-adapted to the marine environment, pinnipeds, unlike the cetaceans, have not totally renounced life on land. During the season of good weather, they gather in large herds on the beaches of the Arctic and Antarctic, both to give birth to the young conceived the year before and to carry out the mating ritual. Each male usually creates a small harem of females that he defends ferociously, engaging in cruel struggles with other males in search of mates.

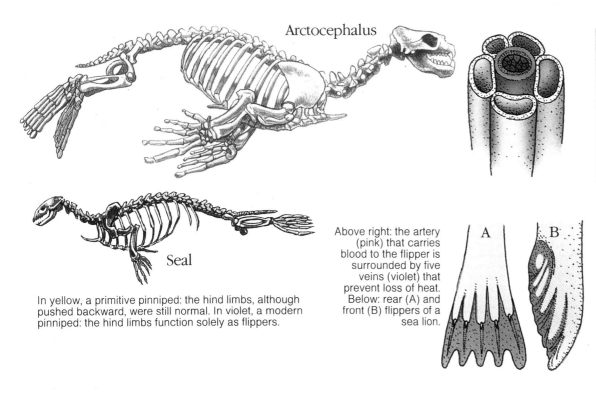

Arctocephalus

Seal

In yellow, a primitive pinniped: the hind limbs, although pushed backward, were still normal. In violet, a modern pinniped: the hind limbs function solely as flippers.

Above right: the artery (pink) that carries blood to the flipper is surrounded by five veins (violet) that prevent loss of heat. Below: rear (A) and front (B) flippers of a sea lion.

Northern elephant seal

Elephant seals take their name from the strange proboscis of the male, a nasal pouch that expands greatly during the mating season.

which emerge the front and rear flippers while the remaining, extremely short part of the limb is contained within the body itself. For this reason pinnipeds are not capable of walking on dry land and must drag their stumpy bodies over the ground or move in small jumps.

The modifications to the skeleton described have appeared gradually over the course of pinniped evolution; in the fossil *Arctocephalus* the limbs were still long and the rear ones in particular, although displaced to the rear, may have been capable of taking the occasional, unsteady step.

DISTRIBUTION AND PROTECTION FROM THE COLD

Pinnipeds can be found in almost all the world's seas, but they are particularly concentrated in the cold waters of the two poles, for their food supply, consisting of fish, cephalopods and crustaceans, is especially abundant in those regions. In such an environment, however, adequate protection against

HUNTING AND ENEMIES

The pinnipeds are as agile in the water as they are awkward on dry land; they can even rival the fastest fish. In fact the latter are only capable of very short spurts of speed and tire rapidly; the pinniped, which has more stamina, can chase its prey for a long while in order to catch it. While the pinniped has no enemies on land, except for the polar bear, which is partial to small and tender seals, and man, there is no lack of enemies to watch out for in the sea, including sharks and killer whales.

RESPIRATION

Like all mammals, pinnipeds also breathe air and therefore have to come to the surface at shorter or longer intervals. It seems that the maximum length of time that they can remain submerged is twenty minutes. On re-emergence these animals may find the surface of the water frozen, but they are able to cut a passage through the ice with their powerful canines.

1) The hunting of fur seals is carried out in many places. This scene, for example, occurs in spring, when the Northern fur seals in their migration to California congregate on several small Aleutian islands to breed: young males are clubbed to death so as not to ruin the pelt. 2-3) The harp seal lives in the Arctic seas and travels long distances beneath the pack ice. When the seal needs to surface it cuts an opening through the ice with its teeth, as is shown in the diagram below. 4) The mane of the male sea lion rivals that of the terrestrial lion. They live in numerous colonies, surrounded by females. 5) Walruses use their canines — true tusks of very hard ivory — to drag their enormous weight onto dry land, to detach bivalve shellfish from the seabed and to engage in fierce combat.

42

Northern fur seal   1

Harp seal   2

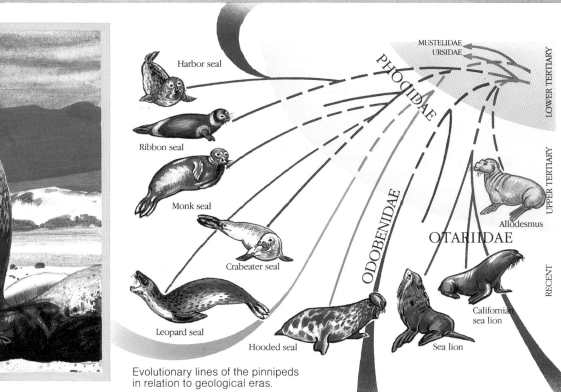

Harbor seal

Ribbon seal

Monk seal

Crabeater seal

Leopard seal

Hooded seal

MUSTELIDAE
URSIDAE

PHOCIDAE

ODOBENIDAE

OTARIIDAE

Allodesmus

Sea lion

Californian
sea lion

LOWER TERTIARY

UPPER TERTIARY

RECENT

Evolutionary lines of the pinnipeds
in relation to geological eras.

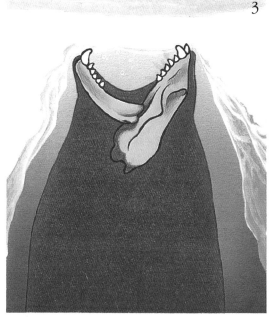

3

5   Walrus

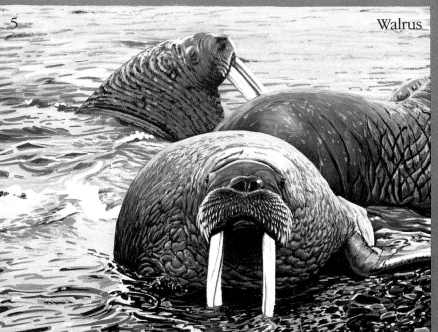

4   South American
sea lion

Humpback whale

Forty tons (36 tons) of ponderous grace erupt as a humpback whale breaches amid the sea off Alaska. First inset: humpbacks sweep their jaws back and forth to trap krill with baleen growing from the pink roof of their mouth. Second inset: during evolution the nostrils of whales moved to the top of the head, forming a blowhole that exhales water-laden air with a characteristic spout.

22. CETACEANS

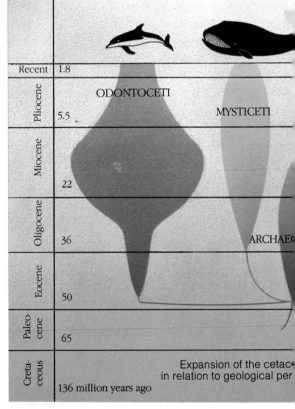

ORIGIN

The cetaceans may also derive from the primitive creodonts, but the early stages of their evolution are unknown to us. In the Eocene Period, 50 million years ago, members of the order were already swimming the seas in the form familiar to us today. Only their teeth were of an archaic type and differentiated into canines, incisors and molars, all of which were to acquire the same conical shape. Yet the evolutionary line of the toothless cetaceans, such as the whales, was already in existence during the Eocene Period.

The cetaceans are divided into three suborders: the *Archaeoceti* now extinct, the *Odontoceti* (dolphins, sperm whales and others), which have mouths full of identical conical teeth, and the *Mysticeti* (baleen whales), which have no teeth but are endowed with close-set horny sheets hanging from the palate, also known as baleen, which filter out their food.

SWIMMING

Of the three orders of placental mammals that have colonized the sea (sirenians, pinnipeds, cetaceans), this is the only one that has totally abandoned any link with the land, conducting all biological functions in the water: feeding, mating, reproduction and so on.

Cetaceans' shape is adapted to aquatic life and the propulsive thrust is provided by the tail and the broad, fleshy terminal flipper. The rear limbs, vestigially present in the embryo, disappear in the course of development, leaving no more than a trace of the femur. Even the forelimb, when it appears in the embryo, is formed along traditional lines, but it is then modified to take the shape of a broad flipper reinforced by a large number of phalanges (just as the flippers of the marine reptiles had been formed millions of years earlier). The head and mouth are extremely large, but the cervical region is very short,

Recent 1.8
Pliocene 5.5
Miocene 22
Oligocene 36
Eocene 50
Paleocene 65
Cretaceous 136 million years ago

ODONTOCETI
MYSTICETI
ARCHAEO

Expansion of the cetace in relation to geological per

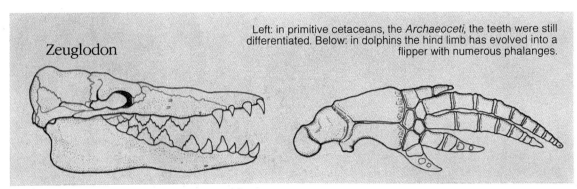

Zeuglodon

Left: in primitive cetaceans, the *Archaeoceti*, the teeth were still differentiated. Below: in dolphins the hind limb has evolved into a flipper with numerous phalanges.

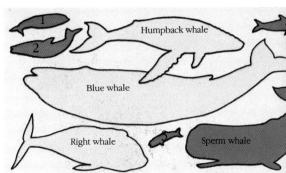

Humpback whale
Blue whale
Right whale
Sperm whale

44

Dolphin

Sperm whale

Among the toothed whales, the dolphin can be found in all temperate seas. It moves in schools, at a maximum speed of 30 miles (50 kilometers) per hour. Inset: the sperm whale is hunted by whalers and used for the production of margarine, cosmetics, animal feeds and fertilizers.

as if these animals had no neck at all: in this respect too they resemble fish.

SIZE

These animals are of considerable size. For an animal that lives habitually in ice-cold waters a larger volume represents an undoubted advantage: a larger body loses proportionately less heat through the skin. The whales can attain exceptionally large dimensions. Indeed the largest living creature ever to have appeared on the earth is the blue whale, which can reach 111 feet (34 meters) in length and a weight of over 143 short tons. (130 tonnes); the largest dinosaur could not have weighed more than 110 short tons (100 tonnes).

Mysticeti, or baleen whales (green) and *Odontoceti,* or toothed whales (red). The whales are represented in their correct proportions. 1) Beluga. 2) *Ziphius.* 3) *Kogia.* 4) *Pseudorca.* 5) *Neobalena.* 6) Narwhal. 7) Pike whale. 8) Killer whale. 9) Dolphin. 10) Pilot whale. 11) *Hyperodon.*

DEFENSE AGAINST THE COLD

The cetaceans are completely hairless, with the exception of a few tactile hairs near the mouth. To conserve body heat they have a layer of fat known as blubber lying beneath the skin, which can be up to 23 inches (60 centimeters) thick. The large quantity of fat that can be harvested from these animals has led to their being hunted with tenacity.

FEEDING AND DIGESTION

The *Odontoceti,* being provided with teeth, hunt even large-sized animals; the killer whales, for example, can attack large whales and devour them in a short period of time. Some dolphins employ a special technique to capture their prey: drawing close to a shoal of fish they emit a sound, as violent as an explosion, that can reach an intensity of 265 decibels (noise becomes unbearable for human beings at 120 decibels). The fish are stunned and easily caught. The

Mysticeti, on the other hand, feed on smaller forms of animal life; their ideal food source is the enormous shoals of shrimp (*Euphausia superba*), commonly known as krill, found in the cold waters of the Antarctic. The sheets of whalebone or baleen that hang from the upper jaw filter shrimp and other small animals out of the water, which are then swallowed.

INTELLIGENCE

The cetacean's brain is very large and rich in convolutions, even more than man's. This is a good indication of their intelligence, confirmed by recent studies of the behavior of dolphins and killer whales raised in captivity. We know that cetaceans are able to communicate between themselves and that they have a marked sense of social cooperation, as they rush to the aid of a companion in difficulty and keep it afloat so that it can breathe. But the actual potential of their brain is still to be determined.

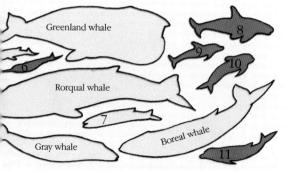

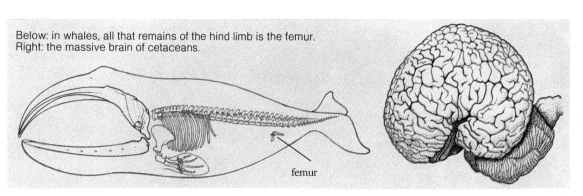

Below: in whales, all that remains of the hind limb is the femur. Right: the massive brain of cetaceans.

femur

23. THE PRIMATES APPEAR

THE *PURGATORIUS*

Our own order has very ancient origins, dating as far back as the final period of the Cretaceous Period, over 70 million years ago. In fact, in that period there lived a small and timid animal whose skull and teeth presented characteristics typical of the *Primates*. This ancient forebear of ours has been given the name *Purgatorius* because of the labor and difficulties involved in the excavations carried out by the scientific expedition that discovered its fossil remains. *Purgatorius* may not be the actual starting-point of the order, but it is certainly the oldest form of primate known to us.

THE *PLESIADAPIS*

About 50-60 million years ago North America was joined to Eurasia by a great land-bridge covered with forests of a tropical or subtropical type. This link permitted the spread of another ancient form of primate, the *Plesiadapis*, into both continents. This precursor was also small, about the size of a squirrel, and must have been able to move rapidly through the branches or along the ground. In the same habitat could also be found the *Adapis*, equally small but perhaps less agile and active.

DIRECT DESCENDANTS

Among living primates there are species that display some striking similarities to the most ancient species, extinct today, as if the process of their evolution had been arrested, allowing them to retain primitive characteristics. The *Tupaiidae* or tree shrews are a good example of an old group of species. Their features are so generic as to be an embarassment to researchers; in fact until not many years ago they were classified among the insectivores, the oldest of all placental mammals.

But more careful examination of the skull and brain has led to promotion of the tree shrew to the ranks of the least evolved primates. Owing to their great similarity, the tree shrews may derive directly from the *Plesiadapis*, making them living testimony to the first evolutionary steps of the primates.

Evolutionary lines of the primates in relation to geological eras and periods. The oldest known representative of the primates is the *Purgatorius*, which lived toward the end of the Cretaceous Period, 70 million years ago. The reconstruction on the right, based on fossil finds of teeth and jawbones, depicts the animal together with two large dinosaurs of the Secondary Era, its contemporaries.

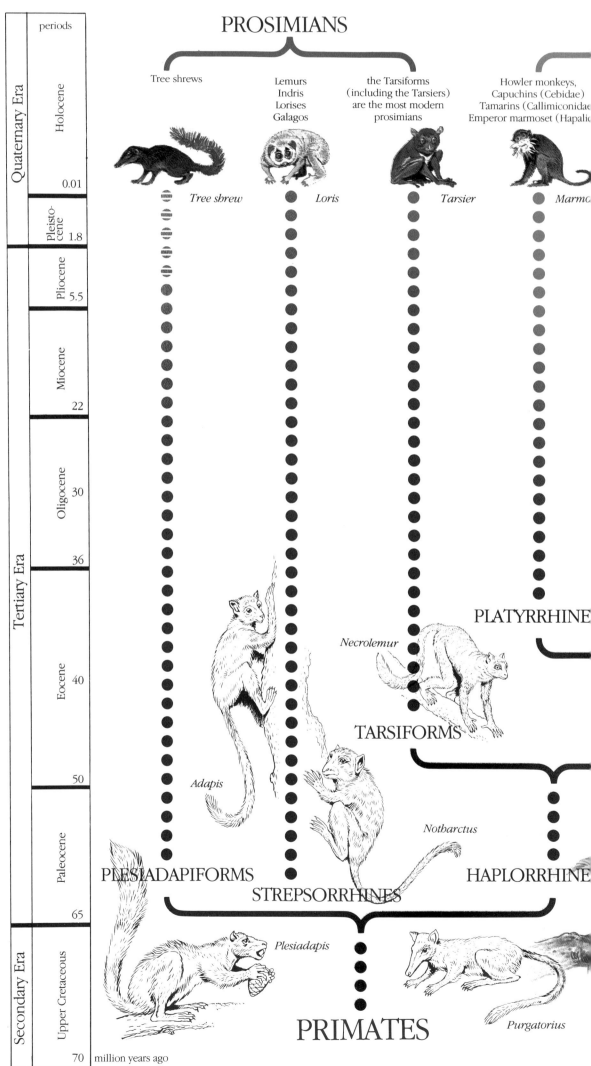

46

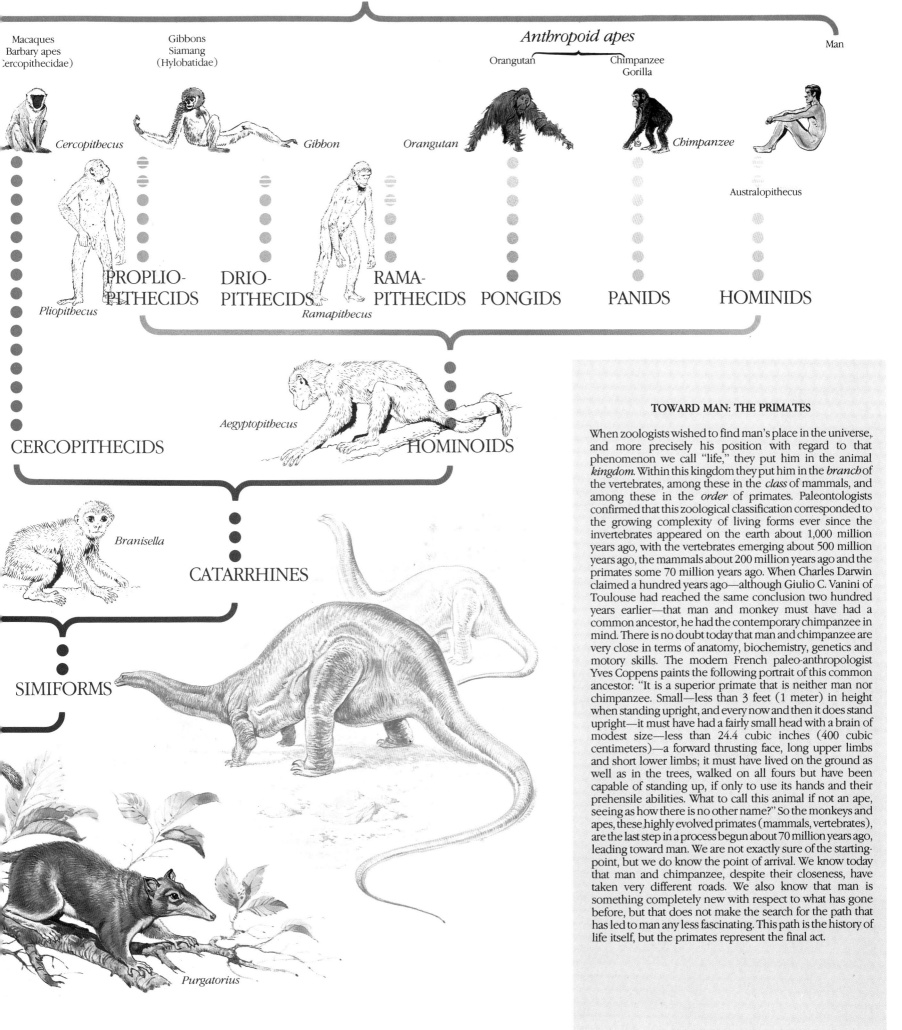

SIMIANS or SIMIFORMS

Macaques
Barbary apes
(Cercopithecidae)

Gibbons
Siamang
(Hylobatidae)

Anthropoid apes

Orangutan

Chimpanzee
Gorilla

Man

Cercopithecus

Gibbon

Orangutan

Chimpanzee

Australopithecus

PROPLIO-
PITHECIDS

DRIO-
PITHECIDS

RAMA-
PITHECIDS

PONGIDS

PANIDS

HOMINIDS

Pliopithecus

Ramapithecus

CERCOPITHECIDS

Aegyptopithecus

HOMINOIDS

Branisella

CATARRHINES

SIMIFORMS

Purgatorius

TOWARD MAN: THE PRIMATES

When zoologists wished to find man's place in the universe, and more precisely his position with regard to that phenomenon we call "life," they put him in the animal *kingdom*. Within this kingdom they put him in the *branch* of the vertebrates, among these in the *class* of mammals, and among these in the *order* of primates. Paleontologists confirmed that this zoological classification corresponded to the growing complexity of living forms ever since the invertebrates appeared on the earth about 1,000 million years ago, with the vertebrates emerging about 500 million years ago, the mammals about 200 million years ago and the primates some 70 million years ago. When Charles Darwin claimed a hundred years ago—although Giulio C. Vanini of Toulouse had reached the same conclusion two hundred years earlier—that man and monkey must have had a common ancestor, he had the contemporary chimpanzee in mind. There is no doubt today that man and chimpanzee are very close in terms of anatomy, biochemistry, genetics and motory skills. The modern French paleo-anthropologist Yves Coppens paints the following portrait of this common ancestor: "It is a superior primate that is neither man nor chimpanzee. Small—less than 3 feet (1 meter) in height when standing upright, and every now and then it does stand upright—it must have had a fairly small head with a brain of modest size—less than 24.4 cubic inches (400 cubic centimeters)—a forward thrusting face, long upper limbs and short lower limbs; it must have lived on the ground as well as in the trees, walked on all fours but have been capable of standing up, if only to use its hands and their prehensile abilities. What to call this animal if not an ape, seeing as how there is no other name?" So the monkeys and apes, these highly evolved primates (mammals, vertebrates), are the last step in a process begun about 70 million years ago, leading toward man. We are not exactly sure of the starting-point, but we do know the point of arrival. We know today that man and chimpanzee, despite their closeness, have taken very different roads. We also know that man is something completely new with respect to what has gone before, but that does not make the search for the path that has led to man any less fascinating. This path is the history of life itself, but the primates represent the final act.

24. THE PROSIMIANS

Perhaps the *Adapis* or some similar creature gave rise to a group of primates that were once very numerous: the prosimians. Even today these animals display markedly primitive characteristics, sufficient to persuade zoologists to relegate them into separate suborders which include the tree shrews, the lemurs, the indris, the lorises, the tarsiers, the galagos and the aye-aye.

DISTRIBUTION

At one time the prosimians were spread throughout North America, Eurasia and Africa, but their numbers were drastically reduced when the more modern simians appeared on the scene with their greater skill at exploiting the arboreal environment. Today they are mainly to be found in Madagascar where they have been able to live in peace without any competition. When this island detached from Africa it was populated solely by prosimians, as the monkeys had not yet appeared, and so it has remained to this day.

Madagascar provides a home to nine-tenths of living prosimians, while a minority of species, such as the loris, the galago (or bush baby) and the tarsier, are distributed over the tropical forests of Africa, India, Indonesia and the Philippines.

FEATURES

The most striking feature of the prosimians is their large eyes, which often shine in the dark owing to the presence of crystals in the retina. This characteristic is typical of the nocturnal animal; in fact, apart from the tree shrew, all the prosimians are highly active only at night, spending their days sleeping in trees in the depths of the forest.

Their diet is varied, including insects, fruit and shoots, but they are prepared to eat almost anything, as in fact are most primates. Their brains are small, and so their intelligence is limited. In general, prosimians are peaceful animals, showing little aggression even among themselves. In the wild each pair presides over a precise territory that is marked out by a secretion from specialized glands; in the lemurs, for instance, this gland is located on the forearm. The odor of this secretion discourages encounters between members of the same species, reducing the possibilities of competition between individuals.

Among the primates, the most primitive group is that of the prosimians. These include the sifaka, belonging to the *Indridae* family, which lives in Madagascar, and the tarsier, found in the Philippines and the Malay archipelago, belonging to the *Tarsiidae* family.

Verreaux's sifaka

Mindanao tarsier

25. PLATYRRHINE MONKEYS

FROM PROSIMIANS TO SIMIANS

About 42 million years ago a new line of evolution arose among the prosimians that was destined for exceptional development: the *Omomyidae*. This may have been the founding group of the suborder of simians that we find distributed throughout Europe, Asia and North America, united in a single continent at that time. During that period, many species, and the primates in particular, were able to move from one continent to another, owing to the presence of tropical-type forests even in high latitudes. At the beginning of the Eocene Period, however, this movement of primates was interrupted; perhaps a change in climate destroyed the forests, leaving in their place broad savannas that could only be traversed by the ungulates and proboscideans. The primates, tied to their lush forests, were split into two groups: one in the Americas and the other in Eurasia and Africa. Their evolution took separate paths: in the American group, that of the platyrrhines or New World monkeys, the animals remained small, with few variations between species and many primitive characteristics; the group which inhabited the other continents, the catarrhines or Old World monkeys, gave rise to a remarkable variety of forms, some of them large, characterized by a well-developed brain. The different destinies of the two groups of primates is a truly strange phenomenon: closely resembling one another at the outset, and living and evolving in similar environments, they produced completely different results.

PLATYRRHINE MONKEYS

The Greek word *platyrris* from which the name of this division of the monkeys derives signifies "broad nose"; in fact these monkeys have very widely separated nostrils and a broad, flat nasal septum. Another characteristic, although not common to all, is the long prehensile tail, capable of gripping branches like a fifth hand. In some species the tail has a large number of nerve endings and is also used as an organ of touch. In comparison to the catarrhines, the platyrrhine monkeys are less lively and intelligent, with the exception of the capuchins.

DISTRIBUTION

The platyrrhines were once widespread not only in North America, where they probably orginated, but in South America as well. This fact poses a considerable problem for paleontologists. How did these monkeys get to South America if the two continents were cut off from one another during the Eocene Period? Perhaps a small colony of platyrrhines was carried to the South on drifting logs uprooted in a storm or perhaps there are other explanations.

The diffusion of the platyrrhines came to a halt in the Oligocene Period, some 30 million years ago, when yet another climatic change caused the tropical forests to disappear from North America, along with all their inhabitants. A similar change in climate almost destroyed the catarrhines in Eurasia.

Today platyrrhines are to be found in the belt of the Americas lying between the tropics, from Mexico to Brazil.

HABITS

The New World monkeys live exclusively in trees; no species, not even among the extinct ones, has ever adapted to life on the ground. Their diet, like that of the majority of primates, is an omnivorous one: fruit, shoots, insects, eggs, small birds, amphibians or, in the absence of anything better, leaves. The platyrrhines are subdivided into three families, the *Cebidae, Callimiconidae* and *Hapalidae*.

CEBIDAE

In the family of cebids we find the capuchin monkeys, the most intelligent of the platyrrhines, which have been extensively studied by ethologists as they are easy to breed and display a wide range of behavior. In proportion to the size of the body, their brain is very large and highly convoluted. The capuchins are capable of using tools, such as stones to break nuts with. Like all monkeys, they take great care of their fur, which they keep clean by removing any insects or foreign bodies that they find in it. This grooming is also performed on the coats of their companions, for the capuchins live in small bands.

CALLIMICONIDAE

This family is made up of a single species of monkey with a completely black coat, Goeldi's tamarin (*Callimico goeldii*). It has been the object of study by specialists as it presents a number of primitive characteristics, as if the evolution of this species had come to a stop ten million years ago. In fact it is considered by some to be a living representative of the monkeys that gave rise to the platyrrhines on one hand and the catarrhines on the other.

HAPALIDAE OR CALLITHRICIDAE

This family of monkeys, commonly known as marmosets, are small, ranging in size from that of a rat to that of a squirrel, and sometimes have brightly colored fur, making them remarkably attractive. The emperor marmoset has enormous whiskers sticking out on each side giving it a strangely austere appearance that contrasts with its playful and lively character.

Right: three members of the group of platyrrhine, or New World monkeys. The capuchin, belonging to the family of *Cebidae*, is widely distributed in the tropical forests of Central and South America. It is often bred in captivity in zoos and institutes of scientific research, for it is the most intelligent of the platyrrhines.
Howler monkeys, which also belong to the *Cebidae* family, take their name from the territorial call of the male. This is so loud that it can be heard for several miles in the jungles of Central and South America, most often at dawn or dusk. They are the largest of the platyrrhine monkeys and, like many of these, use their long prehensile tail as an extra hand when swinging through the branches.
The emperor marmoset, a member of the *Hapalidae* or *Callithricidae* family, belongs to a genus (*Saguinus*) that is distinguished by its great variety in facial appearance. Many species have crests, whiskers and beards in a wide range of colors — although as a group they resemble each other closely. This species in particular owes its name to its long, pale whiskers, similar to those of Wilhelm II, emperor of Germany up until the first world war.

Capuchin monkey

Red howler monkey

Emperor marmoset

The gibbon, a member of the *Hylobatidae* family, swings through the trees like an acrobat.

The orangutan is an anthropoid ape belonging to the *Pongidae* family.

Gorilla

The gorilla is an anthropoid ape belonging to the *Panidae* family. In spite of its menacing appearance, it is extremely docile.

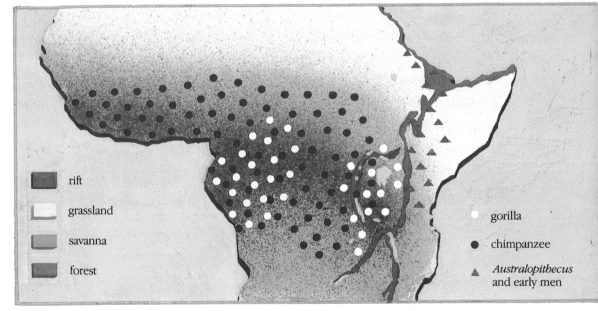

rift

grassland

savanna

forest

○ gorilla

● chimpanzee

▲ *Australopithecus* and early men

Distribution of the *Panidae* (gorilla and chimpanzee) and the hominids (*Australopithecus* and early men) in intertropical Africa about 10 million years ago.

26. CATARRHINE MONKEYS

The oldest fossils of the catarrhines can be dated to around 38 million years ago.

These monkeys evolved in Asia, Europe and Africa, driving the prosimians from the forests. In some evolutionary lines this evolution of the catarrhines led to an increase in the size of the brain, resulting in increasingly refined behavior and intelligence.

The tail is not prehensile; in fact, it is often missing altogether. The nostrils are set very close together, hence the name given to these primates: catarrhine, from the Greek word meaning "drop noses." Their nails are often flat. The thumb and the big toe are opposable, permitting a firm grip on branches, as the

THE DIVISION BETWEEN GREAT APES AND HOMINIDS

All experts in the field are now prepared to acknowledge the relationship between the family of the HOMINIDS (*Pre-Australopithecus, Australopithecus, Homo*) and that of the PONGIDS, the great anthropoid apes of Asia such as the orangutan, and the PANIDS, the great anthropoid apes of Africa, especially the gorilla and chimpanzee. The relationship signifies that hominids, pongids and panids had a common and not very remote ancestor, but the question remains as to how and where the separation took place. Twenty years of research in Africa have established that on no archaeological site in the east and south of the continent can hominid fossils be found together with those of panids, while the latter are distributed in completely different zones (see the map above).

Around ten million years ago the famous Rift Valley formed a true ecological boundary; to the west of it the landscape remained covered with forests which disappeared to the east. The gorilla and chimpanzee, the panids, were to become the rulers of the forest, while hominids would inhabit the more open landscape, better suited to bipeds.

50

Chimpanzee

Close observation of chimpanzees in the wild state in their African habitats presents great difficulties. This is why laboratories of ethology have been set up in a number of European zoological parks, where scientists can study the social behavior of these primates in a partially natural environment. Here we see one of these laboratories in Holland, near the city of Arnhem. Chimpanzees, anthropoid apes belonging to the *Panidae* family, have been extensively studied owing to the emotional ties that link parents and their offspring, and to their ability to learn through imitation and to invent and use very primitive tools.

majority of these monkeys have arboreal habits; however, several species live and reproduce on the ground as well. The history and distribution of the catarrhines is linked to climatic conditions of the tropical or subtropical type. In Europe they have disappeared.

Living catarrhine monkeys are divided up into four great families: *Cercopithecidae, Hylobatidae, Anthropoid Apes, Hominids.* The latter will be described in the next two chapters.

CERCOPITHECIDAE

This family comprises a large number of species which inhabit Africa and Asia, such as the macaques, baboons and mandrills, all familiar types of monkeys frequently encountered in zoos. In the wild they live in communities both in the trees and on the ground, where some are capable of covering short distances walking upright on their hind legs.

HYLOBATIDAE

The predominant characteristic of the *Hylobatidae* is a new way of moving through the trees; the long arms are adapted for grasping branches and swinging from tree to tree. The gibbon's mode of motion is an excellent example of what is known as "brachiation." Among other things, this innovation brought about considerable modifications in the skeleton that would be extremely useful further down the line of evolution leading to man.

ANTHROPOID APES

The name given to this family derives from their close resemblance to man.

The *orangutan* (pongids) lives today on a few Asian islands (Sumatra and Borneo) where it leads a totally arboreal life. Its disposition is mild, even between individuals of the same species and the same

sex. Its survival is threatened because of the gradual disappearance of its natural habitat, but a variety of institutions are concerned with its protection.

The *gorilla* (panids) lives in Africa, and is the largest and most powerful of the apes. It grows up to 8 feet (2.5 meters) in height and can exceed 660 pounds (300 kilograms) in weight. It does not have a very prepossessing appearance and as a result has always been regarded as aggressive and fierce. Nothing could be further from the truth. In the wild the gorilla is a mild and sociable animal; conflict never gets beyond the stage of dirty looks and the odd howl, even where strangers are concerned. This peaceful temperament is associated with an almost totally vegetarian diet.

The *chimpanzees* (panids) also live in Africa, but are much more widely distributed. A great deal of study of the behavior of these animals is going on today, as it presents some remarkably interesting aspects such as the capacity to learn by imitation, to use twigs to collect food, etc.

51

27. THE ROAD TO MAN

In Chapter 23 we saw that the emergence of the primates 70 million years ago represented the beginning of the final stage on the road to man, who is therefore a PRIMATE, HAPLORRHINE, SIMIFORM, CATARRHINE, HOMINOID and HOMINID.

Let us now look at the last two phases of this stage, those of the HOMINOIDS, small primates whose earliest fossils date to about 35 million years ago, and the HOMINIDS, the most highly evolved primates. The hominids are the only family of bipedal hominoids. They habitually walked upright, and are divided into three genera: *Pre-Australopithecus, Australopithecus* and *Homo*.

Here we will make use, in outline, of the description given by the paleo-anthropologist Yves Coppens (using all the geological, paleological and biological data available) of six "personages" who during the last 35 million years have represented stages of the journey towards ourselves. These are *Aegyptopithecus, Proconsul, Kenyapithecus, Pre-Australopithecus, Australopithecus* and, finally, *Homo*. Only the latter would really succeed in expanding beyond the confines of Africa and spreading all over the world.

AEGYPTOPITHECUS

Thus the first actor to enter the stage is *Aegyptopithecus*, whose fossil remains were found in the sedimentary basin of El Faiyûm in Egypt. This is the earliest higher primate that we can classify in the superfamily of the hominoids. The fossils have been dated to about 34 million years ago. This simian already large for its day was a quadruped about the size of a gibbon, a cat or a fox. It lived in groups in the trees and was highly sociable; a skillful climber, its diet consisted of fruit and nuts. Its skull, although modest in size, contained a brain that, as revealed by studies of casts made from the fossil cranium, displays some major changes: the forehead is higher, visual capacity has increased and the sense of smell diminished.

The journey toward the human brain had begun. In fact this simian appears to have been the greatest innovator in the history of evolution, for it was able to adapt to an environment, that of the Nile delta, that had a tropical forest cut through by strips of open land and subject to seasonal climatic changes. For the ancestral tarsiforms it had been impossible to emerge from the great humid forests.

PROCONSUL

Various fossils of the second character in our story, *Proconsul*, have been found in East Africa (Kenya, Uganda). This hominoid lived from 23 to 14 million years ago. Of a size ranging from that of *Aegyptopithecus* to that of a small gorilla, this arboreal quadruped seems to have been a powerful climber, with strong limbs and slow movements.

This simian, which had lost its tail, lived in the forests that covered the slopes of volcanoes and at the same time moved into the more thickly wooded parts of the savanna. Its cranial capacity had risen to 9 cubic inches (150 cubic centimeters) and a genuine auditory canal had appeared. 17 million years ago, *Proconsul* was able to spread into Asia and Europe over the land-bridge that was formed at that time; hence we find fossils of its descendant, *Dryopithecus*, in France as well.

KENYAPITHECUS

We return to Africa to meet our next protagonist. *Kenyapithecus* was discovered by Louis Leakey in Kenya. This hominoid had so many characteristics that resembled those of the hominids that in the beginning Leakey himself gave it the name *Kenyanthropus*. The size of a small chimpanzee, this quadruped was already adapted to spending part of its life on the ground and must have stood upright from time to time. When standing it would have been slightly under 3 feet (1 meter) in height. Its dentition shows us that, unlike the two preceding hominoids, it was able to vary its diet considerably. It ate not only fruit and leaves, but also roots, seeds and perhaps even meat and bones, all food gathered at ground level. *Kenyapithecus*, which often ventured out of the forest into the savanna in search of food, was the protagonist of a great discovery. All of 14 million years ago this predecessor of ours was able to pick up tools similar to the ones depicted on the opposite page, from the ground it explored (Fort Ternan, Kenya). It used them to shatter bones and extract the marrow. Its brain had attained a capacity of 18.3 cubic inches (300 cubic centimeters) and the teeth reveal that it had a prolonged infancy. We are getting closer and closer to man.

skull and reconstruction of
AEGYPTOPITHECUS

skull and reconstruction of
PROCONSUL

skull and reconstruction of
KENYAPITHECUS

52

Scene of life for a group of *Pre-Australopithecus* in the East African savanna.

HOMO SAPIENS SAPIENS

HOMO NEANDERTHALENSIS

skull and reconstruction of PRE-AUSTRALOPITHECUS

AUSTRALOPITHECUS AFRICANUS

AUSTRALOPITHECUS ROBUSTUS (BOISEI)

HOMO HABILIS

HOMO ERECTUS

The oldest tools in the world. Right: stone with worn edges and battered long bone, Fort Ternan, Kenya. Below, left: flaked stones, Omo Valley, Ethiopia.

PRE-AUSTRALOPITHECUS

The following "personages" make up the great family of the hominids, characterized by their bipedalism and the tendency towards increasing development of the central nervous system. In the next chapters we will deal with *Australopithecus* and *Homo*, but here we will meet the fourth actor in our adventure: *Pre-Australopithecus*.

We now enter the subfamily of the australopithecines. A permanent biped, but still an excellent tree-climber, it was not much over 3 feet (1 meter) in height. Its cranium had a capacity of 24.4 cubic inches (400 cubic centimeters) and its teeth already displayed typically human traits, with the canines no longer than the other teeth.

Pre-Australopithecus still lived in a very humid environment, but one that was already cut off from the great forest inhabited by gorillas and chimpanzees. The landscape through which it moved was made up of areas of wooded savanna, much like islands of forest surrounded by great expanses of grassland.

The most famous discoveries connected with *Pre-Australopithecus* are of a female skeleton in Ethiopia, given the name "Lucy," and the one at Laetoli, in Tanzania, where fossil footprints of hominid have been found.

A group of *Homo habilis* in the African savanna, about 4 million years ago. In depicting the first men, along with their social nature and communal life, now evident to archeologists, this illustration sets out to convey their capacity for reflection on the meaning of life and universe.

skull of
HOMO HABILIS
East Turkana, Kenya

Stones worked by *Homo habilis*, found at Olduvai, in Tanzania.

28. HOMO

AUSTRALOPITHECUS

The "road" on which we started in the last chapter now brings us to the fifth character in our story, *Australopithecus*, which inhabited southern Africa from 5 to 1 million years ago. However this population was split into two different lines of evolution: *Australopithecus africanus*, or *gracilis*, and *Australopithecus robustus*, or *boisei*.

The former, which had a more lightweight skeleton, was no taller than 4 feet (1.25 meters) with a cranial capacity of 27.4-30.5 cubic inches (450-500 cubic centimeters). Its general characteristics suggest that it was still in the habit of climbing trees to gather food or to take refuge from predators. Its teeth were strong and its diet was probably predominantly vegetarian, although it could include the occasional small animal.

Australopithecus robustus appeared somewhat later, a little over 2 million years ago, and disappeared after a period of over a million years. This hominid was taller and heavier—5 feet (1.5 meters), 110 pounds (50 kilograms)—and seems to have appeared as an adaptation to a more arid environment with only

a small number of widely scattered trees. Its diet was based on roots, bulbs and tubers.

The australopithecines already made extensive use of tools, such as sticks, bones and stones, the latter probably used to crush bones and extract the marrow. A recent discovery in the Omo valley, in Ethiopia, suggests that they may even have been capable of chipping stones to make cutting tools.

HOMO

We now encounter the last actor in our story, *Homo*. Today we can say that man was probably born in East Africa, before the australopithecines and even the pre-australopithecines had come to the end of their own story. Thus man was a contemporary of *Pre-Australopithecus* for a short period, and of *Australopithecus* for perhaps as long as 2 million years. It is now evident that the australopithecines are too similar to man not to be related to him. Their location in the same part of Africa, with fossils of both hominids found on the same sites, and the fact that the australopithecines are older and less specialized,

means that we must look for the origin of man in an East African australopithecine. It is probably about 5 million years back that we must look for a ramification of the evolutionary line of *Australopithecus* leading to the emergence of a new species: man.

Our character is *Homo*. The fact that he is called *Homo habilis* at the beginning and then *Homo erectus* and *Homo sapiens* does not mean that we are dealing with different species. *Homo* is a single species: his evolution, unlike that of the creatures that preceded him, did not involve a radical biological change but a process of cultural development.

So culture enters the history of the cosmos. Right

54

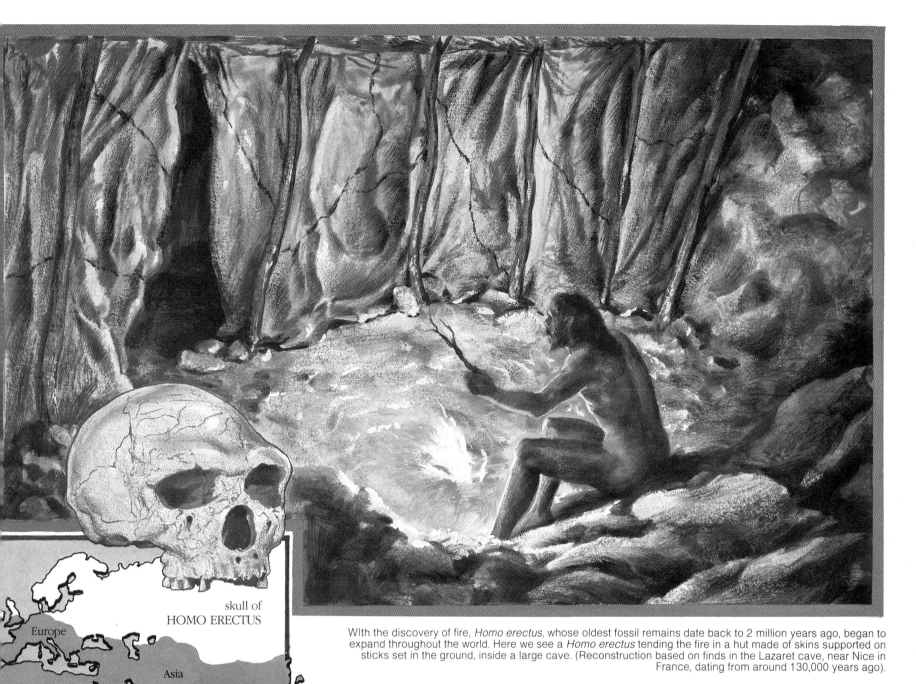

skull of
HOMO ERECTUS

Europe

Asia

Africa

With the discovery of fire, *Homo erectus*, whose oldest fossil remains date back to 2 million years ago, began to expand throughout the world. Here we see a *Homo erectus* tending the fire in a hut made of skins supported on sticks set in the ground, inside a large cave. (Reconstruction based on finds in the Lazaret cave, near Nice in France, dating from around 130,000 years ago).

Area in pink: from Africa, cradle of his origins, *Homo erectus* spread into Asia and Europe.

from the start man is a protagonist who tends not only to adapt to the world that surrounds him, but to adapt the world to his own ends. We might say that man is not just industrious, but that he is a true constructor of reality.

He lives in groups and through the medium of language passes on what he has acquired to others, thereby increasing the level of culture from generation to generation. Man is therefore a *communicative being* and a *social constructor*, conscious of his limits in a fascinating world; but it is also a dangerous world, and so man is *fearful* and *cunning*.

Moreover man cannot avoid asking himself questions about life, cannot help being aware of the gap between his desire to go on living, to grasp reality, to understand where he comes from and where he is going, and his impotence, his physical limits, night, death and the like.

HOMO HABILIS

Thus we call the man who appeared in Africa (Kenya, Ethiopia, Tanzania, South Africa) over 4 million years ago *Homo habilis*. He was not very tall, around 4.2-4.5 feet (1.3-1.4 meters), but with a cranial capacity that attained and in some fossils exceeded 42.7 cubic inches (700 cubic centimeters). His diet was omnivorous, and it is very likely that he hunted small animals which he killed with the tools he made. The environment in which he lived was typical of the savanna. He may have liked to camp close to water courses or lakes, as traces of his camps, revealed by large numbers of stone tools, are often to be found in such places. Investigation of cranial casts also indicates that *Homo habilis* used to communicate verbally with his fellowmen.

HOMO ERECTUS CONQUERS THE WORLD

Fossil remains from less than 2 million years ago begin to display still more advanced characteristics: cranial capacity ranges from 48.8 to 73 cubic inches (800-1,200 cubic centimeters), height has increased and the skeleton grown more massive and robust. This kind of man already stood perfectly erect, and the tools he created were more refined.

Up until 2 million years ago all the events connected with the origin of man had occurred in a relatively small area of Africa. With the appearance of *Homo erectus*, or as it would be more correct to say, when man began to display new cultural characteristics, his expansion throughout the earth began. *Erectus's* great innovation was the control and use of fire, which permitted him to exercise greater sway over his environment. By this means and with his culture, the communities of *Homo erectus* became more and more numerous and he began to emigrate out of Africa. Within a short period of time man not only spread over the whole of that continent, but into Europe and Asia, even reaching many islands by navigation (another new discovery).

55

Neanderthal burial at
Tesik-tas, in Central Asia.

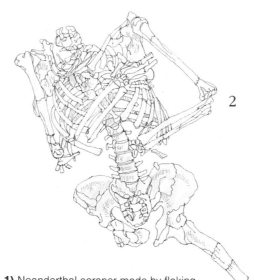

1) Neanderthal scraper made by flaking.
2) Arrangement of the skeleton of a Neanderthal man in the burial-site at Kebara, Israel.
3) Neanderthal skull found at La Chapelle aux Saints, Corrèze, France.

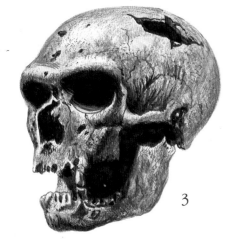

29. # MODERN MAN

We describe ourselves today as *Homo sapiens sapiens* (with a distinct lack of humility, seeing as how we call ourselves doubly wise). Modern man appeared on the earth about 40,000 years ago. As with the transition from *Habilis* to *Erectus*, however, the appearance of *Sapiens sapiens* was not a sudden event but took place through the progressive modification of *Erectus*.

BIOLOGICAL EVOLUTION AND CULTURAL EVOLUTION

Having finally reached our goal, let us linger for a few moments to take a look at the final stages in the evolution of man, from 5 million years ago to the present day, from the appearance of *Homo habilis* to *Homo sapiens sapiens*. The skeletal modifications that have taken place along this line of evolution mainly affect the cranium, or at least it is this feature that seizes the imagination.

Within the span of a few million years the volume of the brain increased from the 30.5 cubic inches (500 cubic centimeters) of the oldest forms of *Homo habilis* to the 91.5 cubic inches (1,500 cubic centimeters) of our own cranium—although that of the Neanderthal variety of *Homo sapiens* even verged on 97.6 cubic inches (1,600 cubic centimeters). Thus the increase in the mass of the brain was extremely rapid, tripling over a short period of time. How was this possible? A recent hypothesis suggests that traditional biological evolution was accompanied by a process of evolution based on culture. That is to say, *Homo habilis* invented, with his ability to modify the nature of things, a technological culture that was of help to him in the different stages of his life. Yet this new creation did not remain an end in itself, but was constantly being modified. To put it more simply, a chimpanzee may discover that tasty ants can be gathered with the help of a twig and by imitation this

Top: a prehistoric ice-age artist painting the walls of a cave in France. Left: the Venus of Vestonice, found in Czechoslovakia, was modeled about 20,000 years ago out of a plastic material made of powdered ivory and clay.

method of collecting food spreads throughout the community, but without ever being modified. In man the transmission of culture takes place through both imitation and verbal communication, but above all it is in continual and progressive evolution. There is therefore a close connection between the brain that makes plans and the utilization of the technology that results from them. The premium on the greater efficiency of tools is a premium on the better, larger and more efficient brain. This is in turn capable of coming up with more sophisticated and effective techniques. So cultural evolution, the exclusive prerogative of man, influences biological evolution and shapes its anatomical characteristics. In its turn biological evolution improves culture.

NEANDERTHAL MAN

The problems posed by this group of men have always proved difficult to solve. The Neanderthals appeared on the earth roughly 400,000 years ago, emerging in the Middle East, from where they spread

56

into Europe, then Siberia and perhaps across the Bering Strait to become the first inhabitants of North America. Their cranial capacity ranged as high as 97.6 cubic inches (1,600 cubic centimeters)—superior to our own!—and they possessed a definite spirituality, as is demonstrated by their burial places and tombs. Neanderthal man was in fact the first to bury his dead, adorning them with flowers.

The reconstruction of the appearance of Neanderthal man has undergone considerable changes as new finds have been unearthed. The earliest drawings depicted them as squat, ape-like figures covered with hair. Time has gradually refined them, culminating in the most recent reconstructions in which the Neanderthal is depicted as an extremely civilized man, even elegant in his features, and above all with a highly intelligent expression. The end of Neanderthal man coincided with our own appearance on the earth, 35,000 years ago.

HOMO SAPIENS SAPIENS

In the same regions inhabited by Neanderthal man, and perhaps even following the same routes, appeared *Homo sapiens sapiens*. As has already been explained his origins can be directly connected with *Homo erectus;* in any case he is definitely not a descendant of Neanderthal man, who appears to represent a separate and sterile branch of the continuous line of evolution *Homo habilis — Homo erectus — Homo sapiens sapiens*. On the arrival of the latter Neanderthal man was forced to give way. There may have been conflict between the two forms of *Homo,* or there may just have been an absorption and fusion of the two. In some regions the fossil remains dating from around 30,000 years ago present characteristics of the two types, whereas in others this fusion seems not to have taken place.

A NEW CULTURE

The arrival of *Homo sapiens sapiens* coincides with more refined techniques for the making of tools, not only out of flint but also of bone, while social life became more highly organized, partially in order to cope with the climatic difficulties of the period. Complex works of art also began to appear, such as statuettes and paintings on the walls of caves. The practice of honoring the dead also continued, enriched with new elements, expressing a clear awareness of death and the desire to transcend it. Around 10,000 years ago in the Middle East, modern man made a radical change in his living habits, turning from a hunter and occasional gatherer of fruits, tubers and the like, into a farmer and breeder of animals. This innovation, immediately successful and rapidly spreading to the rest of the world, brought a huge increase in the number of individuals, as well as the creation of the first cities, the invention of writing and, unfortunately, conflict between groups and cities and the resulting first wars. From this moment on man's cultural development proceeded at a dizzying pace.

Yet man, while he has shown himself capable of great inventions, is equally capable of deeds of great destruction. Alongside splendid civilizations we find wars and brutalization.

Each time that man sets himself up as the sole lord of the planet and of his fellow creatures it is a prelude to disaster. As long as he continues to question his origin and his fate, or to recognize his thirst for the infinite along with his own limits, man will be able to go on living, to be Writer, Artist, Builder, Father or Mother, and not to fall into inhuman ways of life.

With the diffusion of agriculture, about 8,000 years ago, man's life underwent a radical change. This scene is set in the vicinity of an Alpine village in Europe, around 500 B.C. Man used the cart as a means of transport and dressed the fields with manure.

The classification of man in the animal kingdom

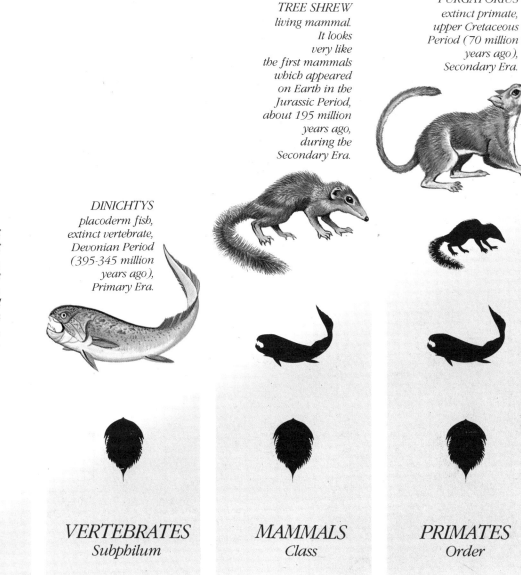

TREE SHREW
*living mammal.
It looks
very like
the first mammals
which appeared
on Earth in the
Jurassic Period,
about 195 million
years ago,
during the
Secondary Era.*

PURGATORIUS
*extinct primate,
upper Cretaceous
Period (70 million
years ago),
Secondary Era.*

DINICHTYS
*placoderm fish,
extinct vertebrate,
Devonian Period
(395-345 million
years ago),
Primary Era.*

**DALMANITES
LIMULURUS**
*trilobite,
extinct
invertebrate,
Silurian Period
(435-395 million
years ago),
Primary Era.*

ANIMAL
Kingdom

VERTEBRATES
Subphilum

MAMMALS
Class

PRIMATES
Order